Waiting for the Lord's Day
Devotional Readings Anticipating Sunday

By the same author
Chorando por Brasil: Crôncias de um Pastor que Olhou para trás
(Memoir in Portuguese)
This Week at Home: Devotional Readings between Sundays
(Lectionary Year B)
Sunday Is Not Enough: Devotional Readings through the Week
(Lectionary Year C)

In Memoriam
Myron Flugstad
(March 25, 1951-August 22, 2016)
my brother
who learned the prayers
and heard the Bible stories
with me around the family table.

Waiting for the Lord's Day
Devotional Readings Anticipating Sunday

Joel Mark Flugstad

Lawler Street Book Concern, LLC
2016

Copyright © 2016 Joel Mark Flugstad.
All rights reserved. This book or any portion thereof may not be reproduced or used in any manner whatsoever without the express written permission of the publisher except for the use of brief quotations in a book review or scholarly journal.

The Scripture quotations contained herein are from the New Revised Standard Version Bible, copyright © 1989 by the Division of Christian Education of the National Council of the Churches of Christ in the U.S.A. Used by permission. All rights reserved.

Cover Photo:
Reformation Day, 2016
Trinity Lutheran Church, Oklahoma City

First Printing 2016

ISBN   978-0-578-18711-2

Lawler Street Book Concern, LLC
Oklahoma City, OK
lawlerstreetbooks@ gmail.com

Contents

I. Advent, Christmas and Epiphany	1
II. Lent	33
III. Easter	49
IV. Pentecost	69
V. Still Pentecost	93
VI. Even So, Come, Lord	117

Preface

I grew up in a family where daily Bible reading and prayer was a constant feature of household life. This custom, typical of Norwegian Pietists and their spiritual descendants, may seem strange to Christians of other traditions. In any case, I think it is a salutary practice that should be encouraged.

A Lutheran pastor once told me that the reason some Lutheran pastors used to visit families in their homes was to check up on their devotional practices. I have not been as bold or nosy as that, but I have from time to time suggested that Christians could benefit from the practice of daily Scripture reading and prayer, not only individually but as a family.

The short meditations in this book were originally written when I was pastor of Our Lord's Lutheran Church in Oklahoma City. I began writing these almost on a whim without any long term project in mind, with the idea that they could be of use to families in their devotional life at home. The readings in this book correspond to the Sunday readings appointed in the *Revised Common Lectionary**, Year A. I hope the reader understands that 'the Lord's Day' in the title refers not only to Sunday but to the Great Eschatological Day of the Lord as well.

--jmf
Willow Creek, Oklahoma City
All Saints Day, 2016

The Revised Common Lectionary, © 1992 Consultation on Common Texts.

I. Advent, Christmas and Epiphany

JOHN THE BAPTIST FINDS A REASON TO HOPE

In jail the prophet has a pang of doubt.
"Are You the One?" he asks, "or must we wait?"
He fears his daring work was all for naught.
"Has God another longed-for candidate?"
John's vivid image painting God's Great Day
Of harvest, threshing, castigating fire
Declares "Messiah comes; prepare His way!
His footsteps tell the time is drawing nigher."
With God great things are not as one expects.
While one proclaimed eternal banishment
Kind deeds reveal the One Whom God elects
Brings healing, wholeness, life, not punishment.
  So John was not far off to say, "Come, see
  The Lamb who deals with our iniquity."

SOMETHING NEW
... put on the Lord Jesus Christ (Romans 13:11-14; v. 14).
The life swept clean by repentance needs to be filled with something that works for righteousness, lest the demons return (Matthew 12:45). Just as you pull a coat over your shoulders on a December morning, now "Put on the Lord Jesus Christ." Let his righteousness be all the adornment and decoration you will need. It is his gift to you. Let it warm you and protect you and you will find it a transformative experience. *Sweep my life clean, Lord Jesus, and let your Spirit work in me the works of the day and of the light.*

A WAKE UP CALL
"Keep awake" (Matthew 24:36-44; v. 42).
Days zip by, and then years, like the electric poles along the highway, and we are coaxed into drowsiness and dullness of senses. Suddenly the Lord himself taps us on the shoulder to bring us back into the present moment. Keep awake! Living in the New Day of Jesus Christ, sustained by grace, we are fully aware of our discipleship. We have neighbors to serve. There is comfort and hope to be extended. All this in joyful waiting for the inauguration of the glorious rule of our Lord Jesus Christ. *Gracious God, I pray for awareness for service and witness, always in joyful expectation.*

PRAY FOR PEACE
Pray for the peace of Jerusalem (Psalm 122; v. 6).
In the Name of God wars are fought, blood is spilled and hatred is nurtured from generation to generation. Pray for the peace of Jerusalem! And of Gaza! And of Baghdad and Kabul and Aleppo! And wherever hearts are heated by injustice, whether ancient or modern. Those who bear the Name of Jesus, the Prince of Peace, should be the first to lay down arms and plead with all on every side for peace. *Lord,*

like your servant Francis let me, too, be an instrument of your peace; in Jesus' Name.

AND STAY AWAKE
"Keep awake" (Matthew 24:36-44; v. 42).
The unexpectedness of our Lord's appearing is the stimulus that discharges adrenalin into our hearts and souls. The possibility from moment to moment of the coming of Christ is the incentive for witness and service in Jesus' Name. What seems to be a delay lures us into complacency. Delay, however, is simply a time of grace that allows for the working out of God's mission and purpose among us. *Heavenly Father, help me to say 'Come, Lord Jesus!' in heartfelt expectation.*

DISARMAMENT
. . . swords into plowshares (Isaiah 2:1-5; v. 4).
When the armies were approaching Jerusalem and fear gripped the hearts of God's people, the prophet talks of peace! We might ask ourselves whether it is arming ourselves in fear or transforming weapons into useful tools that most reveals faith and trust in God. The promise of God through Jesus Christ is that, finally! On That Day! The science of war will be forgotten and the war colleges will become training academies for agronomists. *Dear God, help me not to be afraid to urge peace among all people; for Jesus' sake.*

THE RESTING SPIRIT
The spirit of the LORD shall rest on him (Isaiah 11:1-10; v. 2).
Jesus is the fulfillment of God's promise proclaimed through the prophet Isaiah. The Spirit of God rested on Jesus at his baptism. When we were baptized into Christ, the Spirit of God rested on us as well. The Spirit of God is both restful and energizing, giving us both relief from the restlessness of our lives as well as stirring us up for love and witness. The Holy Spirit gives us "wisdom and understanding . . . counsel and might . . . knowledge and the fear of the Lord." And in the

Spirit the fear of the Lord is our delight. *Dear God, by your Spirit resting on me, stir me up to faith, hope and love, for Jesus Christ's sake.*

PATHS THAT NEED STRAIGHTENING
"Bear fruit worthy of repentance" (Matthew 3:1-12; v. 8).
Repentance is not only saying "I'm sorry." The fruits of repentance are changed behaviors. If there are misunderstandings that need to be clarified, we do not let them fester. If our self-interest stands in the way of serving our neighbor, we re-order our priorities. We examine our own life to avoid in us what irritates us in others. When we look at ourselves honestly, we see it is not the Lord's paths that need straightening but ours. Repentance will lead us on the straight way to God's grace in Jesus Christ. *Lord God, by your Spirit resting on me, smooth the rough places in my behavior.*

THE KING'S DUTY
May he defend the cause of the poor (Psalm 72:1-7; v. 4).
Christians apply this psalm to Jesus, the King of kings and Lord of lords. It is also a prayer for all who are in authority over us. It is the king's duty to "defend the cause of the poor . . . deliver the needy . . . judge with righteousness and justice." Supremely God does all this through the work of Jesus Christ. While we wait for That Glorious Day of Our Lord Jesus, we pray that God's will may be done "on earth as in heaven" through the work of those in authority, and that it may be done through us as well. *Gracious God, by your Spirit resting on me, make me aware of how I can love and serve my neighbor in need.*

A LONG WINTER
Welcome one another, therefore, just as Christ has welcomed you (Romans 15:4-13; v. 7).
A construction worker was hastening back to his work station, passing by co-workers without stopping to chat. His boss chided him. "You

can't just walk by people," the boss told him. "It's going to be a long winter." There are theological or technical "marks of the church" (the Gospel proclaimed, the sacraments administered, etc.), but there are also practical markers of the church of Jesus Christ. Welcoming each other, speaking kindly to one another, is one of them. We're in this together until the Lord comes to welcome us into his hospitable kingdom. We can't just walk by each other without stopping to chat. *Lord Jesus, by your Spirit resting on me, give me a friendly conversation.*

THE DIFFERENCE
. . . to live in harmony with one another (Romans 15:4-13; v. 5).
The population of the church differs from the general population only insofar as it is governed by the grace of the Lord Jesus. Christians have divergent political views; Christians offend each other, sometimes maliciously, often unwittingly, just as their non-Christian neighbors might. We are held together by the bonds of grace. We prove to be gracious people when we bear another's burdens, and bear with each other in spite of issues that otherwise would divide us. *Heavenly Father, by your Spirit resting on me, help me to live harmoniously with the dissonance around me.*

DISAPPOINTMENT, MAYBE
"Are you the one . . . ?" (Matthew 11:2-11; v. 3).
When expectations are not realized, there may be doubt or disappointment. Jesus was not the Messiah that most people were waiting for, maybe not even the Messiah we had hoped for. No revolution; no Dark Day of Judgment; no king's palace. Instead, a cross, and resurrection, and a promise of a return. All of this signaled by great deeds of healing, cleansing and restoration. There comes a time when we realize life has not turned out as we had expected. When reality does not coincide with our hopes, we will wait eagerly for the Promised Return of our Lord Jesus to see what kind of

fulfillment God has in mind. *Dear God, I pray that your purpose for me may be fulfilled through Christ my Lord.*

OUR RETURN

. . . the ransomed of the Lord shall return . . . (Isaiah 35:1-10; v. 10).
We languished under the power of petty gripes, or the unwillingness to forgive, or the turning of the head to avoid another's greeting. We were in captivity of our own making and didn't know it. Then, the Prince of Peace lifted us from the bondage of old attitudes and set us gently down in his kingdom, where forgiveness is real and means reconciliation with God and neighbor. It was a high price, but God is motivated by love, and we come into God's Presence with singing and everlasting joy. *Gracious God, help me to see my own captivity, and by the power of your grace, to walk out and leave it behind.*

MAGNIFICAT ANIMA MEA

He has scattered the proud in the thoughts of their hearts (Luke 1:46-55; v. 51).
Such a revolutionary song for gentle Mary! If the Gospel were business as usual there would be no good news. The Life growing in Mary's womb challenges all our human institutions, ideas and achievements. There is justice for the downtrodden; there is resolution for our anxieties; there is forgiveness for sinners. All this is accomplished by the Life initiated by God and nourished by Mary. Therefore we sing with the Mother of Our Lord, "My soul magnifies the Lord." *Dear Lord, tune my voice to sing with Mary.*

THE RIGHT TIME

The farmer waits for the precious crop . . . (James 5:7-10; v. 7).
When one has done all that can be humanly expected, the one who plants can only wait and trust God to produce the harvest. The seed has been planted. The crop will mature. Jesus will appear at the right time for the harvest. Meanwhile, there are prayers to be said,

neighbors to be served, comfort to be given, and peace to be made. While we wait there is even time for amendment of life! In everything, we trust God for the harvest. *Heavenly Father, give me an eagerness for the return of the Lord Jesus.*

OVERTURNED EXPECTATIONS
"And blessed is anyone who takes no offense at me" (Matthew 11:2-11; v. 6).
It is hard to imagine how anyone might be offended by Jesus, unless we pay attention to what he actually teaches us. John the Baptist came breathing dire threats. Jesus comes to restore us in the fullest possible measure. We know how to love our friends and bear grudges against our enemies. Jesus teaches us to love our enemies. In Jesus the Messiah the expectations are overturned. What we get, by grace, is God's rule that transforms our sinful nature, bending and shaping it to conform to the image of Christ. *Lord God, by the power of your grace, help me to receive the teaching of Jesus with joy.*

GOD'S CONSTANT REFRAIN
"Do not be afraid . . ." (Matthew 1:18-25; v. 20).
There was a disturbing new development in Joseph's life. We also know the sudden pang of anxiety when we are surprised by circumstances over which we have no control. God's constant refrain in Scripture is this: "Do not be afraid." Isaiah heard it: "Do not fear . . . you are mine" (Isaiah 43). The shepherds heard it: "Do not be afraid . . . I am bringing you good news of great joy . . ." (Luke 2:10). Over and over, "Do not be afraid" is God's word for us. *Be near me, Lord Jesus, I ask thee to stay / Close by me forever, and love me, I pray* (John Thomas McFarland, 1851-1913).

A NEW AWAKENING
. . . when Joseph awoke from sleep . . . (Matthew 1:18-25; v. 24)
When we awake in the morning the same duties and needs await us that were on our minds as we fell asleep. When righteous Joseph

awoke he realized it was more than a dream. There were new duties and responsibilities that were very real indeed. To take Mary as his wife, as the angel commanded, meant taking care also of the Life growing within her, a Life "conceived of the Holy Spirit." When we open our eyes in the morning we should not think that nothing has changed. In the power of the Holy Spirit there is New Life growing within us as well, "Christ in us, the hope of glory" (Colossians 1:27). *Lord, I would like to feel your gentle kick within me.*

EMMANUEL (or is it 'Immanuel'?)
. . . his name shall be called Emmanuel . . . (Matthew 1:18-25; v. 23).
Emmanuel (sometimes spelled with an "I" –ask your pastor to explain!), the Evangelist tells us, means 'God with us.' This is companionship at a sublime level. Whether there is one inhabited world in this universe or countless, the God of all creation is 'with us.' Because of Emmanuel, days of joy are filled with a sanctifying Presence, and days of sorrow or pain are also filled with a Love 'that will not let us go.' It is companionship beyond friendship. *When I look at the stars, I am thankful for your Presence in this small world as well.*

SAVIOR
. . . he will save his people from their sins (Matthew 1:18-25; v. 21).
Sin may be a dismal word to think about. What is even worse, however, is living with the very real consequences of sin. Even if we believe in forgiveness, words and actions as well as inactions can haunt us forever. Jesus saves us from our sins. Let the bitter memories serve as warnings about future behavior. But let Jesus be our Savior who lifts us up and out of our sin and makes us righteous. *Glory to God in the highest!*

A Different Song

. . . when the goodness and loving kindness of God our Savior appeared . . . (Titus 3:4-7; v. 4).

The righteous fury of the prophets has faded away, and now comes the Word of God in a different tone and sung in a different key. The world, restless from a sense that all is not right, hears the lullaby sung by Mary and finds its rest in Jesus. Forgiveness of sins for sinners, comfort for the afflicted; confidence for those fearful of the present or future; and peace between enemies and peace with God—for all this Jesus is born. *Gracious God, in the noise of my own thoughts, let me hear the melody of your New Song, in the key of Jesus.*

Christ the Savior

"I bring you good news of great joy" (Luke 2:1-20; v. 10).

In Jesus, God has confronted the problem of sin and death and evil, and has prevailed. There is good news for those who feel the weight of sin, because Jesus is forgiveness and empowerment for the good life. The birth of Jesus is good news for those who struggle with the snares and tricks of the evil one, because Jesus means freedom from sin's power to convict, condemn and control. Even at death's door, in Christ the best is yet to come. *Heavenly Father, let me taste that great joy of Jesus!*

The Light of the World

The people who walked in darkness have seen a great light (Isaiah 9:2-9; v. 2).

Jesus Christ is the Light of the World: the Light no darkness can overcome! Jesus shines in our hearts to see both ourselves and our neighbors as we really are: loved by God, the one needing to be forgiven as much as the other; all uniquely blessed with personality and gifts to enrich our common life. In Jesus we see things as they really are. *Shine on me, Lord Jesus!*

The Visible Word
The Word became flesh . . . (John 1:1-14; v. 14).
The invisible sound that brought all things into being has become visible and now participates in the material substance of creation. God became one of us, and this never ceases to astound and amaze. The visible word, Jesus Christ, takes all the guess work out of it. We have seen and heard what God has in mind for us. Chiefly God calls us to believe in the One Whom God has sent. *Jesus, my Lord, and my God!*

The New Israel
"Out of Egypt I have called my Son" (Matthew 2:13-15; v. 15).
If Israel is God's 'son' who, through disobedience and unfaithfulness, is a disappointment to God, Jesus, through his obedience and faithfulness to the will of the Father, is the fulfillment of God's expectations for his people, and therefore the fulfillment of our hopes as well. Jesus has joined us in our captivity, and by his death and resurrection embodies the New Israel and claims us as God's sons and daughters. *Heavenly Father, grant that I may bring honor to your holy Name.*

December 26
Saint Stephen, Deacon and Martyr
. . . they . . . covered their ears . . . and rushed together upon him (Acts 7:51-60; v. 57).
The story of how the diaconate was established is written in chapter six of Acts. Stephen is the first named of the deacons (6:5) whose responsibility it was to see to the daily distribution of food to the Christian widows. The word 'deacon' means 'one who serves.' Stephen also undertook his witness not only in deed but in word as well. It is his sermon in chapter seven charging his listeners with rejecting the Righteous One that gets him in trouble. They stone him and as he dies he prays, "Lord, do not hold this sin against them" (v. 60). Saint Stephen's Day is referred to in the carol *Good King Wenceslaus* who *look'd out / on the Feast of Stephen* , i.e., on December 26. The king

notices a poor man gathering wood on the cold winter day. He and his page personally deliver food to him.

December 27
SAINT JOHN, APOSTLE AND EVANGELIST
If we confess . . . God will forgive . . . (1 John 1-2:2; v. 1:9).
There is some risk in confessing one's sins. It is at the very least embarrassing, even if it is only our silent confession before God. To say "I am a sinner" is only to acknowledge one's humanity, which requires no spiritual courage at all. But to say "I am guilty of such and such a sin" is to really make oneself vulnerable. The call to repentance, or confession, however, always occurs in the context of God's grace and promise of forgiveness in Jesus Christ. The Evangelist, the bearer of Good News, tells us plainly that those who risk the vulnerability of honest confession will find absolute peace with God. *Lord God, please hear my confession. And I need to hear your word of forgiveness, in Jesus' Name.*

December 28
THE HOLY INNOCENTS, MARTYRS
Rachel . . . refused to be consoled (Matthew 2:16-18; v. 18).
The violence and cruelty of which human beings are capable is beyond description. Hearts are still filled with agony on account of unspeakable acts of inhumanity that we have heard of even in recent times. The mothers of Bethlehem—Rachel—"weeping for her children" refused to be consoled. God the suffering Parent also refuses to be consoled about wickedness on this tiny planet. Jesus—the one who saves his people from their sins—comes with grace to release us from our hatred, to heal our sorrows and take away our bitterness. *O God, you know the pain that refuses to be consoled. Let me be healed of my hatred and sorrows; for Jesus' sake.*

A WARMING WIND
He sends out his word and melts them (Psalm 147; v. 18).
The human race often seems like a snowstorm out of control. Winds are blowing every which way, and we get lost between the barn and the house. Nevertheless hearts grown cold against God or neighbor cannot resist the warmth of God's Spirit whispering gently to revive us. Like ice in springtime that turns into a lively and flowing stream, so God softens our hardened attitudes and entrenched behaviors, releasing us for service and devotion. *Gracious Spirit, when a harsh word is on the tip of my tongue, grant me grace to use a kind one instead; for Jesus' sake.*

January 1
THE NAME OF JESUS
Whatever you do . . . do everything in the name of the Lord Jesus (Colossians 3:12-17; v. 17).
On the first day of the New Year, as humans mark time, honoring Christ is our organizing principle. We study hard to honor Christ; we work hard to improve the common good in the Name of Christ; we love family and friends to glorify Christ; in the Name of Jesus we love the unlovely; in Jesus' Name we enter in to our recreation. Doing everything in Jesus' Name will help us to stay out of trouble. *Holy God, I begin this day and this year in Jesus' Name.*

IT IS ONLY when one knows the unutterability of the name of God that one can utter the name of Jesus Christ.
        –Dietrich Bonhoeffer, in *Letters and Papers from Prison.*

A SPECIAL BABY
. . . the only Son . . . has made him known (John 1:14-18; v. 18).
"What's so special about Baby Jesus?" the child asks her mother on Christmas Eve. "Let-there-be-Light" has taken on flesh and blood. God in diapers. God skinning his knee. God hungry, thirsty and tired. God in the wilderness struggling hand-to-hand with the devil. In making

God known the Son of God has also shown us who we are. Christ "became sin" so that we might become the "righteousness of God" (2 Corinthians 5:21). This is a special Child, indeed. *Lord Jesus, remind me again that you have made me 'the righteousness of God.'*

January 6

THE EPIPHANY OF OUR LORD

They knelt down and paid him homage (Matthew 2:1-12; v. 11).
First they worshiped! At the Name of Jesus, "every knee should bend," as the very old hymn says (Philippians 2:10). First we worship, not to fulfill an obligation—Christ is the fulfillment of the law—but to acknowledge that our life, our well-being, our salvation, come to us by grace through Jesus Christ. Without Christ we have no gifts to offer at all. When grace breaks through we sense a fullness that is not ours. Then, "We give thee but thine own." *Lord Jesus Christ, we praise thee, we bless thee, we worship thee . . ."*

WELCOME, JESUS!

The light shines in the darkness, and the darkness did not overcome it (John 1:1-18; v. 5).
Jesus Christ is the Light of the World: the Light no darkness can overcome. Against the light, darkness has no chance. We ourselves have experienced this. When the light of Christ casts its glow into the unlit places in our souls, there is healing, forgiveness, and the dark thoughts scurry away. We welcome Jesus Christ the Light of the World into our lives, again and again. *Shine, Jesus, shine! And scare away the darkness in my life.*

A CLEAR WORD

He declares his word to Jacob, his statutes and ordinances to Israel (Psalm 147:12-20; v. 19).
We do not always appreciate the Word of God that has been declared to us. The Bible is thick and complicated, full of unfamiliar and perhaps unfathomable words and expressions. The Word, however, is

really quite simple and clear. The Word is Jesus Christ, through whom God reveals his love for us and through whom we have been forgiven and given life. God's Word will always show us how much we need Jesus Christ, and point us in that direction. *Lord God, I will always let you have the last Word.*

CHILDREN OF GOD

. . . he gave power to become children of God, who were born, not . . . of the flesh . . . but of God (John 1:10-13; vv. 12-13).
Sometimes we like it and sometimes we don't, but no one can choose one's parents or family. It is true physically, and spiritually as well. If we say it was God who chose us, rather than the other way around, it becomes a source of great comfort, and boasting loses its place. We can be glad, therefore, that it is God who gives birth to our faith and makes us God's children. Whether we are "a handful" for God, or charmingly obedient, we belong to our heavenly Father. *Gracious Lord, grant that I may never be ashamed to name you as my heavenly Father; for Jesus sake.*

IN THE BEGINNING WAS THE WORD, AND THE WORD WAS WITH GOD, AND THE WORD WAS GOD
--John 1:1

GRACE, ONCE MORE

We have all received grace upon grace (John 1:14-18; v. 16).
If we are made of flesh and blood we need no convincing that the grace of God has piled up for us. Our sins are forgiven; the embarrassing mistakes of the past are gathered up into the love of God; and our rebellion and foolishness have been taken up into the cross. Even when difficulties have arisen, we have seen that "the Lord

will provide." God centers our lives in Jesus Christ, because this is where we will meet the grace of God. *Your grace has abounded for me, Lord God, more than I can count or tell. So let it count for transformation and be telling through my life of faith in the Lord Jesus.*

The Baptism of Our Lord
A LONG LINE AT THE JORDAN RIVER

"I need to be baptized by you" (Matthew 3:3-17; v. 14).

The Holy One approaches and, in spite of our piety, religiosity and favorable reputations, we sense our tremendous inadequacy. Nevertheless, we have been baptized in the Name of Father, Son and Holy Spirit. Forgiven, cleansed, we have been raised with Christ to newness of life (Romans 6). It is the Happy Exchange. Jesus stands in line with sinners to take their guilt into himself and to give them his righteousness. *Lord Jesus, help me to remember and to reclaim the baptismal gift, day by day.*

THE BELOVED SON

"This is my Son, the Beloved . . ." (Matthew 3:13-17; v. 17).

Other than one's spouse, it is hard to imagine a love greater than a parent's love for a child. The voice from heaven is filled with love beyond human telling. God is pleased with Jesus the Beloved Son. This is love so great the cosmos can barely contain it. Yet there is another love, also bursting the limits of human imagination. God's love for the world is unveiled in the death of the Beloved Son. *You have filled with world with your love, Lord God. Let it fill my heart as well.*

GLORY!

. . . *and in his temple all say, "Glory!"* (Psalm 29; v. 9).

After the whirlwind, there is ice and then there is sun. Awed by phenomena too great to control, too mysterious to fully understand, we can only say, "Glory!" When the shepherds and wise men are put back in their storage boxes, we remain with words too useless, too feeble even to be uttered. In the presence of God-dwelling-among-us, Jesus Christ of Nazareth, we can only gasp a frail "Glory!" In response to the love of God shining through the life, death and resurrection of the Beloved Son we can only sputter, "Glory!" In the temple the Holiest One deigns to be contained within the very ordinary, and we say, "Glory!" *Glory to you, our God; glory to you.*

Our Judge

. . . ordained by God as judge of the living and the dead (Acts 10:34-43; v. 42).

If we could choose our own judge we would choose the same one God has chosen, Jesus Christ our Savior! The One Who "went about doing good and healing all who were oppressed by the devil" reveals the true nature of judgment. It is the power of evil that is judged. In the end Jesus, in the victory of his resurrection, will free us from every selfish, self-destructive, wicked and degenerate thought and deed, so that we may live with him in "righteousness, innocence and blessedness." *I read / In a book / That a man called / Christ / Went about doing good. / It is very disconcerting to me / That I am so easily / Satisfied / With just going about.* –Toyohito Kagawa.

The Obsessive Gardener

A dimly burning wick he will not quench (Isaiah 42:1-9; v. 3).

In former times if an oil lamp was left unattended it would manage to extinguish itself. In modern times if someone brushes against a houseplant a bent stem might be left to wilt away. Whether through inattention or by injury inflicted by another, both in ancient as well as modern times, there are seasons of spiritual dullness. Do not be afraid of those times when the flame of faith threatens to flicker out. The Lord Jesus tends to our needs like an obsessive gardener. When we are bruised and hurting his grace heals and strengthens. When we drown in doubt and despair, Jesus stands beside us, extending a hand, ready to be grasped by those who cry out, *"Save us, Lord, for we are perishing."*

MAKING A DIFFERENCE
"I have labored in vain . . . (Isaiah 49:1-7; v. 4).
Over against the cold, harsh world, it is difficult to "make a difference." Working for justice or to alleviate poverty, trying to convert a friend or just trying to be a more loving person, responsible to God and neighbor, requires more stamina than most of us can muster. When we are about to give up, the cross of Jesus comes into view, hiding as it does a power and glory beyond description. With the cross comes the promise, "My grace is sufficient for you, for power is made perfect in weakness" (2 Corinthians 12:9). Resting in this promise, we continue to do our work as Christians, knowing that in the Lord our labor "is not in vain" (1 Corinthians 15:58). *Lord God, help me not to wallow in my discouragement but to rest in your grace, for Jesus; sake.*

SOLIDARITY WITH SINNERS
. . . that he might be revealed to Israel (John 1:29-34; v. 31).
They trooped out to the Jordan River. First ordinary folk, then Pharisees and Sadducees and even soldiers. Then came those who thought it was the trendy thing to do. In the midst of that procession of pilgrims, One stands out, One Who was oddly out of place but Who stood in line with sinners. Jesus is shown to be in solidarity with sinners on the one hand and the agent of transformation on the other, as the One Who takes away the sin of the world. *O Christ, thou Lamb of God, who takest away the sin of the world; have mercy upon us and grant us thy peace.*

Testimony
Were I to proclaim them . . . (Psalm 40; v. 5).
The psalmist is eager to give his testimony. For many of us "giving one's testimony" about what God is doing in our lives does not come easily. It may even frighten us a little to think that God might be ***doing something*** to direct our lives one way or another. "The wondrous deeds of the Lord" begin, for us, with Jesus Christ. God's "thoughts toward us" resulted in the Word Incarnate, the Redeemer from sin, whose Spirit leads us into newness of life. *Father in heaven, enliven my sensibility to what you are doing in my life and where you are leading me; in Jesus' Name.*

Spiritual Gifts
Not lacking in any spiritual gift . . . (1 Corinthians 1:1-9; v. 7).
Every Christian without fail and without exception has an array of spiritual gifts according to God's plan and purpose, and for the good of the body of Christ. Every Christian congregation will look a little different because the gifts are different, but there is also a similarity among Christian gatherings because all serve the one Lord Jesus Christ. Spiritual gifts bring us to faith in Christ and help others in their own faith and life. Whatever is useful to enhancing faith and for generating love is a spiritual gift. *O Holy Spirit, I ask for the gift of genuine rejoicing over the gifts you have given to others, and for the gift of boldness to use the gifts you have given me; all for Jesus Christ's sake.*

Behold the Lamb of God
"Here is the Lamb of God . . . " They followed Jesus (John 1:35-42; vv. 36, 37).
John the Baptist was intriguing enough that people left the comfort and convenience of the city to go out to the wilderness surrounding the Jordan River to hear what he had to say and to do whatever he told them to do. What power! John, however, knew his mission. His purpose was to lead people to Christ. "Here is the Lamb of God," he

said to his disciples. And off they went . . . to follow Jesus! The purpose of every Christian witness is to point others to Christ. *Lord God, as your servant John pointed people to Christ, enable me, too, to follow Jesus and not look back.*

January 18
THE CONFESSION OF SAINT PETER
. . . by the name of Jesus Christ of Nazareth (Acts 4:8-13; v. 10).
The true disciple and saint always gives the glory and honor to the Lord Jesus Christ. A man who had been lame was "walking and leaping and praising God" (Acts 3:8). It would have been absurd for Peter and John to claim credit for it. The Name of Jesus, crucified and risen, is the power in our lives that lifts us up from doubts, fear, anxiety, pettiness, and especially from the grave heaviness of life's most pressing issues. *In the Name of Jesus, O God, grant me strength to get up and walk in discipleship.*

THE MIND OF CHRIST
. . . that you be united in the same mind . . . (1 Corinthians 1:10-18; v. 10).
Some Christians will prefer the red carpet for the chancel, and some like the blue. We will even grant that Christians can hold conflicting political views. Neither carpets nor politics are of ultimate concern, however, unless they conflict with what *is* of ultimate concern, namely the lordship of Jesus Christ. Where the thinking of all Christians converges is in "the same mind" we have in Christ Jesus. The mind of Christ will always challenge the thinking of our own minds. *Heavenly Father, may I value the mind of Christ ahead of every other kind of mind, open or otherwise.*

THE CROSS WINS THE DAY

. . . and not with eloquent wisdom, so that the cross of Christ might not be emptied of its power (1 Corinthians 1:10-18; v. 17).

When there is tragedy the pundits want to be theologians, muttering about "where is God in all this?" It never occurs to them that God might just be in the middle of human suffering. The Apostle of the Cross says, "May I never boast of anything except the cross of our Lord Jesus Christ" (Galatians 6:14). In the end it is neither sophisticated philosophy nor shallow speculation that wins the day, but the Suffering Servant of God, Jesus Christ, and his cross and resurrection. Let the cross always have center stage. *Lord God, I pray that my life and witness may find their power in the cross of Christ.*

FEAR

Whom shall I fear? (Psalm 27; v. 1).

Sometimes it is a perceived danger that frightens, and sometimes the frightening thing is the proposed solution to the perceived danger. In either case, fear provokes us to overreact. "When evildoers assail me . . ." I can react, returning evil for evil. Or I can trust that, whatever else happens, "the LORD is my light and my salvation." There are prudent things one can and should do in the face of danger (whether real or imagined), but the first thing is to trust the goodness of the Lord revealed in Christ's resurrection victory. *Gracious God, when fears are all around, let me be the witness for trust; in Jesus' Name.*

GOD'S RULE

. . . the kingdom of heaven has come near (Matthew 4:12-23; v. 17).

Jesus and his contemporaries knew the power of worldly kingdoms. Empires mix justice with injustice, loftiness of spirit with foolish adventure. Regulations and laws seem to favor some while the victims of exploitation are powerless. Jesus proclaims another kingdom, where God rules. In Jesus himself, God's rule has come near. Here, sinners experience grace, the exploited are vindicated, and justice is not a desire for revenge spoken through clenched teeth, but God's victory over sin on the cross. *Father in heaven, your kingdom come and rule on earth, and rule also in me.*

SOMETHING TO TALK ABOUT
"I will make you fish for people" (Matthew 4:18-23; v. 19).
Are these the Seven Most Feared Words in the Bible? They are if we put the task of evangelism ahead of discipleship. It is not a technique, or "How to" or "tools." No one can fish for people who has not first heard the Two Words, "Follow me!" It is the overpowering, thrilling call of Jesus and our response to live in the power and presence of Jesus that gives us something to talk about. *Lord Jesus Christ, I am not sure whether your call is thrilling or threatening. Help me to hear your Word as it really is.*

January 25
THE CONVERSION OF SAINT PAUL
You have heard . . . of my earlier life (Galatians 1:11-24; v. 13).
We are naturally suspicious of people who change sides. Paul changed sides, confusing friend and foe alike. Paul's life shows that transformation is possible and actually happens. Each of us has an "earlier life," whether last year or merely yesterday. God's grace in Jesus Christ is constantly renewing us and reshaping us to conform to the image of God's Son, Jesus Christ. If there is a difference between earlier life and current life, it is a reason to give glory to God. *Dear God, the former life is always close at hand. Raise me up, always, to newness of life in Christ.*

February 2
THE PRESENTATION OF OUR LORD
She began to speak about the child . . . (Luke 2:22-40; v. 38).
Every person's experience of Jesus is unique. Ancient Anna told people that this Child has to do with "the redemption of Jerusalem." Simeon saw Jesus as "a light to the Gentiles." Another might

experience Jesus as "the love that will not let me go." Someone else might know Jesus as the One who restores my true nature. *Lord Jesus, you are many things to different people, and your grace is perfect for each one.*

Have a Blessed Day: Part I
GIVING UP POWER TO CONQUER

"Blessed are the meek . . ." (Matthew 5:1-12; v. 5).

Legions of angels were at his disposal to overthrow Romans, local politicians, and The Establishment. Instead, Jesus came into Jerusalem, meekly, mounted on a donkey. The meek are those who could respond to threats with convincing power but don't, preferring to conquer enemies with love. Jesus came to overcome sin, death and devil, but not with the destructive weapons the world so fondly embraces. God's power was revealed as love in the weakness, shame and suffering of the cross. Jesus promises blessing for those who follow in His Way. *Lord Jesus, make me so strong that I may become meek.*

Have a Blessed Day: Part II
A DIFFERENT KIND OF HUNGER

"Blessed . . . those who hunger and thirst for righteousness . . ." (Matthew 5:1-12; v. 6).

Injustice, whether on the large scale or on the personal level, is never an abstract idea. Injustice always hurts. There are two sides to this, of course, ours and theirs. If we are guilty of sin against God or neighbor, there is a price to pay and we hope for forgiveness. If, on the other hand, our neighbor deprives us of justice we grind our teeth and wait for lightning to strike. God's righteousness is revealed in the forgiveness of sins. We lay our injustice on the cross of Christ, and that is where we put our neighbor's injustice as well. Since we all know the gnawing emptiness of sin, we all will have our fill of God's righteousness. *Gracious God, in anticipation of the Great Banquet when we will be filled, I pray that the righteousness of Christ may fill my life today.*

Have a Blessed Day: Part III
WHO, INDEED?

Who . . . ? Those who walk blamelessly . . . (Psalm 15; vv. 1, 2).

We cower, trembling, before the dreaded question, "Who may abide?" because we recognize our unworthiness. We are not helpless, however. We are made righteous by God's grace and strengthened by the Holy Spirit to buck up and do what is right according to God's will. "What is right" in God's eyes is always a challenge to our nature and understanding. Slander, getting even, exploitation, all these come naturally. Discernment of God's will in ambiguous situations always taxes our spirituality. By grace we dwell on God's holy hill. By grace we are empowered to walk blamelessly. *This time, Lord Jesus, it is I knocking on the door of your tent, asking if I may abide.*

Have a Blessed Day: Part IV
IN THE HEART

"Blessed . . . the pure in heart . . ." (Matthew 5:1-12; v. 8).

It all begins in the heart: careless words, evil intentions, lust, slander, the insatiable desire for more and more. The trouble begins within, in the heart. It is there also that God begins His Work with us. The Spirit of God gives us a clean heart and a new spirit through the grace of Jesus Christ. There is room for God in clean hearts. They used to sing this song in Junior Choir: *Into my heart, into my heart, Come into my heart, Lord Jesus; Come in today, come in to stay.*

Have a Blessed Day: Part V
MAKING PEACE

"Blessed . . . the peacemakers . . ." (Matthew 5:1-12; v. 9).

Making peace is always hard work, and not always our first idea. Wars between nations and between people drag on and on, which should turn our heart to believe that Jesus was absolutely serious when he promised blessing to peacemakers. Peacemaking is not without risk. God made peace by the blood of his Son Jesus. Disciples of Jesus will understand that peace ultimately requires sacrifice. Jesus does not promise blessing for those who prevail over their enemies, but for those who work for peace. *Heavenly Father, I pray for a vocabulary of pleasant words in hostile environments, for Jesus' sake.*

LIGHT

"... *let your light shine* ..." (Matthew 5:13-20; v. 16).

It is not a matter of learning how to generate light. Light is what God in Christ has made us. "You *are* the light of the world" [emphasis added]. We are light because we are Christ's. We are light because we have been forgiven, reconciled to God and neighbor, raised to new life by the grace of the Lord Jesus. We are light because we know how to love our enemy and forgive "those who sin against us" and really mean it. We are light because God sends his grace and mercy through us to the world around us. "Hide it under a bushel? No!" *Lord Jesus, let there be light! Your light, shining in me and through me, to fulfill your purpose for me.*

THE LAW

"I have come not to abolish but to fulfill ..." (Matthew 5:13-20; v. 17).

Whether the Law is easy or hard depends on our relationship with Jesus Christ. The grace of the Lord Jesus brings us to a new understanding of God's will. The Law restrains from murder and theft, but grace teaches that insulting is the same as murder and dishonesty the same as theft. We cannot live like this unless we have first been touched by grace to free us to know the Law as God's way to live as fully complete and satisfied human beings. *God of accountability, I know I fall short of your glory; I pray that the Spirit of Jesus may fulfill your law in me, that you may be glorified!*

Our Security

The righteous . . . are not afraid of evil tidings (Psalm 112; vv. 6, 7).
Christian people are not unaware of danger. Christians, however, turn first in trust and confidence to the Lord Jesus Christ whose resurrection has defeated sin, death and the power of evil. Some may be influenced by demagoguery and extremism of one kind or another. Our witness is generosity, tranquility, and rational responses to complicated issues. Our security is the God who loves us in Christ Jesus. *Lord God, I am often afraid; help me to trust you always for all things; in Jesus' Name.*

A Watered Garden

Your ancient ruins shall be rebuilt (Isaiah 58:1-12; v. 12).
In the cycles of life there are times of building, then decline, then rebuilding. Relationships flourish and flounder. Our faith burns brightly one day and the next we can barely manage to say "Thank you, Lord, for the new day." For people who know something of devastation, God shows the way and makes a promise. "If you remove the yoke . . . the speaking of evil . . . offer food to the hungry . . . you shall be like a watered garden . . . your ancient ruins shall be rebuilt." *Father in heaven, I thank you for the tasks of love you have given me to do. I am trusting you to rebuild whatever is broken in my life.*

Christian Attitudes

. . . spiritually discerned (1 Corinthians 2:14-16; v. 14).
There are some things that cannot be taught as though they were scientific formulas or historical facts. Being gracious with brutes, being patient with prickly personalities, exchanging a heart of stone for a warm and generous heart—these are things that only the Spirit can teach, and they are learned spiritually. Christian attitudes are learned

by living day by day in the grace of the Lord Jesus Christ. *Holy Spirit, teach me the Way of Christ my Lord.*

STOP THE LITURGY!
". . . first be reconciled to your brother or sister . . ." (Matthew 5:21-26; v. 24).
We worship with great solemnity and interruptions are awkward and spoil the mood. Yet it is as though Jesus would say, "Stop the liturgy! Don't even take up the offering! First be reconciled." Reconciliation between people who are crosswise with each other is more important than worship, more important even than the offering. There is a reason we press the pause button during worship. It gives us a chance to be reconciled before we present our offerings. *Lord Jesus, give me courage to ask for forgiveness from the one I have offended.*

LUSTY STALLIONS
" . . . already committed adultery with her in his heart" (Matthew 5:27-32; v. 28).
Jesus is not naïve about the human race. Jesus knows how clever these lusty stallions can be to circumvent the intent of the Commandment. All sin begins within, in the heart. The purpose of the Law is to affirm and protect all relationships, and in this case, God's Law protects the marriage bond. It all begins with the way we look at people. Jesus addresses his words to men, but this is an equal opportunity Commandment. *Correct my vision, O God.*

NO LOOPHOLES
You have commanded your precepts to be kept diligently (Psalm 119:1-8; v. 4).
Our human nature chafes against the intent of God's Law. We are experts at discovering the loopholes, strict about the letter but careless about the spirit or the purpose of the Law. The Law puts a protective fence around all relationships—our relationship with God, first of all, and relationships with family and neighbor as well. When God's precepts are diligently observed relationships thrive and life is a

delight. Thanks be to God for Jesus Christ who fulfills, in us and for us, God's Law. It is in Christ that life turns out to be a delight. *Heavenly Father, for Jesus; sake, help me to love and obey your Law.*

CALLED TO A SPIRITUAL LIFE
. . . as long as there is quarreling among you, are you not of the flesh? (1 Corinthians 3:1-9; v. 3).
We are spiritual people. We are also fleshly people, and often the desires of the flesh are more interesting than the impulses of the Spirit. It is easier to quarrel than to make peace and forgive. It is just exactly when we remember that we are called to a spiritual life that the Spirit of Jesus Christ enables us to do what the flesh cannot do. If we let offenses pass us by without retort or recrimination, it is not we but Christ in us who makes it happen. *Holy Spirit, nurture in me the mind of Christ.*

A LIVING ORGANISM
. . . God gave the growth (1 Corinthians 3:1-9; v. 6).
Beyond water and sun and good soil there are countless interactions within a plant that work together for growth and productivity. The church is a living organism, the Body of Christ. Each member contributes in ways that only God fully understands to the health and growth of the Body. Each one is essential—only God knows why!—to bring about the results that God intends for the church in a particular place. In this mystery to God be the glory! *I am amazed, Lord God, that so many odd types are needed for the ecology of your church. By your Spirit help us to grow together into the fullness of Jesus Christ.*

EVANGELICAL CHRISTIANITY
"Love your enemies and pray for those who persecute you" (Matthew 5:38-48; v. 44).If we start reading Matthew's gospel to find out how to really follow Jesus, we might not get far beyond chapter 5. If anyone wants a

snapshot of what a Christian life might look like, this verse will do it. The Christian imitates Christ who, on the cross in love for God's enemies, prayed for his executioners. If you dare step into this picture, you will have discovered evangelical Christianity, good news both for those who are fleeing from God as well as for those who, searching for God, have lost their way. *Make me bold, heavenly Father, to follow Jesus.*

A Test of Discipleship

. . . leave them for the poor and the alien (Leviticus 19:9-18; v. 10).

Here is an example of how the economy of the kingdom of God works. Unlike human economic systems, based on strict measures of work and reward, in God's kingdom there is first of all concern for the needy. In worldly economies whatever falls into my hands is mine. In God's economy whatever falls into my hands is a test of my discipleship. Surely God is pleased when we are concerned for the well-being of our neighbor, and in doing this we will experience the joy of Jesus. *Every day, Lord, by your goodness, my discipleship is being tested. I pray for the joy of sharing; in Jesus' Name.*

What Matters

Turn my eyes from looking at vanities (Psalm 119:33-40; v. 37).

There is a time for small, mindless pleasures. Recreation is also part of the goodness of the Lord. We do not need to be reading the Bible all the time. Every conversation does not need to be theological, although there is nothing wrong with talking about the Bible and one's faith. But keeping things in perspective, we will know that whoever wins the game today will not matter tomorrow. What matters is that in all our seriousness and in all our diversions we are witnesses for the grace of God in Jesus Christ. *Father in heaven, let your grace be sufficient to lighten all my burdens.*

THE FOUNDATION
. . . that foundation is Jesus Christ (1 Corinthians 3:10-11; v. 11).
Some groups exist to "do good," or "to make this world a better place." Christians organize themselves in congregations on account of Jesus Christ. Sometimes Christians are not sure what the next step might be in their life together, but if they are built upon the foundation of Jesus Christ, the shape of their life and mission will be determined by that same Foundation. In any construction project there is always a reason for building on the Foundation. *Lord God, I pray that my life may be built in a disciplined way upon the Foundation of Jesus Christ.*

PAYING ATTENTION
Do you not know that you are God's temple and that God's Spirit dwells in you? (1 Corinthians 3:16-23; v. 16).
Perhaps we knew it, but maybe we have forgotten. This reminder comes to give us great joy. The motivation and direction for our lives are already built in, by God's Spirit. It is not a case of self-starting, or aimlessly searching for a path forward. It is the Spirit of Jesus Christ, given to us in baptism, whose indwelling works faith in us and illumines the way of discipleship. It is always a matter of paying attention. *Holy Spirit, remind me, again, of your dwelling place; for Jesus Christ's sake.*

NOT FORGOTTEN
"See, I have inscribed you on the palms of my hands" (Isaiah 49:13-16; v. 16).
God does not need cheat sheets, but *just in case!* –there are the names, written in cosmic-sized letters, not to help God remember but to comfort his people. Sooner or later everyone, giants in the faith as well as the rest of us, will have thoughts that echo the despair of Zion, "The Lord has forsaken me." Then we see our names in that kind and generous Hand, and we remember that God is faithful to his children. "Rejoice that your names are written in heaven," Jesus said (Luke 10:20). *Dear Lord, it gives me joy to know that you never forget my name.*

THE NECESSITY OF FORGIVENESS
I am not aware of anything against myself, but I am not thereby acquitted (1 Corinthians 4:1-5; v. 4).
Those convicted of crimes and misdemeanors may have a deeper sense of God's grace than many who cannot brag about blatant and egregious sins. To claim the *necessity* of forgiveness when we are "not aware of anything against me" may be harder to swallow than if someone could accuse us of a sin worthy of scandal. The point of "justification by faith" is that it is God's righteousness, not our own, that we claim in Jesus' Name. *For Jesus' sake, dear God, forgive my sins, especially the ones unknown to me.*

FOUNTAIN OF TRANQUILITY
I have calmed and quieted my soul (Psalm 131; v. 2).
Our days may be agitated. We awake with the "to do" list already scrolling by. Something unexpected happens and plans are abruptly changed. Our first instinct is to rush, leap, act, or perhaps panic. God's Holy Spirit, source and fountain of tranquility, always responds to our needs. The first movement of calming our soul is itself a response to the Spirit's assurance that in the power of the resurrection of Jesus, all will be well. *Holy Spirit, I rest in your tranquility.*

STANDING WITH THE GUILTY
. . . the Lord . . . will bring to light the things now hidden . . . (1 Corinthians 4:1-5; v. 5).
Judgment works both ways. Rarely, in a dispute, is one person alone responsible. In any case, we cannot know all the details even if we are the victim of harm to body or soul. A Christian virtue, and a sign of the Spirit's Presence, is to allow God to be judge, however righteously indignant we might have a right to be. In the final analysis, it is Jesus who comes to judge "the living and the dead," and with all the guilty we stand before the throne of grace. *Your judgments are always righteous and true, Lord God.*

Striving
"But strive first for the kingdom of God and his righteousness . . ." (Matthew 6:24-34; v. 33).
The kingdom of God is not to be confused with any earthly kingdom, however noble or beloved. Nor is the kingdom of God to be confused with any ideal outlined by noble human minds. Earthly utopias are always imperfect because they are based on human justice which is always imperfect, approximate, and tilted to the side or the other. The righteousness (i.e., justice) of God is shaped by grace. Where God rules by grace there is power to transform lives according to God's will for us in Christ Jesus. We strive for this kingdom because what is missing in ours we find in God's. *Let your grace transform me into a citizen of your kingdom, heavenly Father.*

The Transfiguration of Our Lord
"This is my Son, the Beloved, with whom I am well pleased. Listen to him" (Matthew 17:1-9; v. 5).
The spotlight shines on Jesus, bringing clarity to our faith and life. Everything else on the stage of our little lives is obscured by the blinding light of a few thousand thousand watts illuminating Jesus Christ, drawing our attention to him alone. The demands of each day, painful memories of silliness or past sins, apprehension about the "Way of the cross"--all these merely clutter up the stage. The spotlight draws us to follow Jesus, wherever he leads. *Lord Jesus, let me hear your words, "Get up and do not be afraid."*

Waiting
"Come up to me on the mountain, and wait there" (Exodus 24:12-18; v. 12).
God calls and we come—to worship, to our devotional time, to a small group—eagerly, but often disappointed if nothing extraordinary happens. Waiting in the presence of God, however, is never "ordinary" time. Watchful, expectant waiting will always be part of

the life of a disciple. God will speak when God is good and ready, and when we are ready to hear what God has to say. *How wonderful it is to wait quietly in Your Presence, gracious God.*

CLEVER MYTHS
Men and women, moved by the Holy Spirit, spoke from God (2 Peter 1:16-21; v. 21).
In our day and age people seem free to invent their own "cleverly devised myths," taking bits and pieces of religious ideas from here and there according to what suits their fancy. Our faith, however, is bound to God's self-revelation in Jesus Christ, and to Scripture as faithful witness to that revelation. Through the witness of many "men and women" the Holy Spirit directs our hearts and minds to place our faith for life and salvation in Jesus Christ. *Thank you, Lord God, for the faithful witnesses you have sent my way.*

HARD WORK
"Get up and do not be afraid" (Matthew 17:1-9; v. 7).
Boundless courage and energy come our way when we sense God's presence. Then, suddenly, the sensation disappears and rapturous faith turns into hard work. Today we may achieve success in our family or work, or maybe it will be "one of those days." There are bound to be disappointments in the hard work of faithful living. Jesus Christ encourages us to get on with our lives and says, "Do not be afraid." *On the way of the cross, Lord Jesus, I am strengthened by your presence.*

II. Lent

ASH WEDNESDAY

This day by springtime calendar decreed
Begins with lingering frivolity
And ends with sorrow, counting each misdeed,
With solemn thoughts of our mortality.
"Remember you are dust" is hard to bear,
And harder still, "To dust you shall return";
A brighter place, in forty days is there,
A death defeating day for which we yearn.
The penitential season comes along
And stirs the sandy desert Lenten path;
The clinging dust of words and deeds gone wrong
Will not release except by cleansing bath.
  When washing is the dusty pilgrims' need,
  Baptismal water makes them clean indeed.

SOLEMNITY

The Lord is king; let the peoples tremble (Psalm 99: v. 1).

The solemn trumpets on Ash Wednesday portend the most solemn of days when our Lord Jesus Christ takes on our mortality and dies. We are summoned today to tremble before the mountain of God. The God we fear, or don't fear, has come in Jesus Christ to love us, to suffer with us, to forgive, reconcile and restore us, and to make us friendly once again with God. "Sometimes it causes me to tremble." *Fill my heart, awe-inspiring God, with the right kind of fear, that I may love you with all my heart; for Jesus' sake.*

CRAFTY
. . . the serpent was more crafty than any other wild animal . . . (Genesis 3:1-7; v. 1).
The problem with law, especially religious law, is that it encourages casuistry, and casuistry brings out the craftiness in us all. We are experts at redefining the requirements. What we need is not a good lawyer who can work the technicalities but an attitude adjustment so that "we may delight in your will and walk in your ways." It is the grace of the Lord Jesus that frees us from the constraints of the law and enables a willing and upright spirit to live in the righteousness of God. *Lord God, help me to give up the need to make excuses, and to trust instead in the power of your grace to make me whole; in Jesus' Name.*

OBJECTS OF WORSHIP
"Worship the Lord your God and serve only him" (Matthew 4:1-11; v. 10).
As disciples of Jesus Christ, we need to be absolutely clear on what might possibly constitute objects of worship in our lives, and therefore become rivals to the Lordship of Jesus Christ. House, car, job, country, family; collections, hobbies or pastimes of sundry kinds (maybe 'Sunday' kinds as well); life style or way of life, political party or ideology . . . Whatever our heart attaches itself to is our idol, Luther said. Scripture is clear. We can only have one God. It is the God revealed through our Lord Jesus Christ whom we worship and serve with singleness of heart and purpose. *Gracious Lord God, help me to see whatever in my life might rival my loyalty to you; in Jesus' Name.*

COVERING UP AND COVERED
Happy are those to whom the LORD imputes no iniquity (Psalm 32: v. 2).
The irony of sin and justification is that those who claim they have nothing to hide will waste away through their "groaning all day long," while those who reveal what they have been hiding find that their sins

are covered by the grace of the Lord Jesus Christ. Cover up, and you are on your own. Reveal what you have stored in the depths of our heart, and the Lord Jesus covers you! *Lord God, I want to be honest about those things down in the depths of my heart. I ask you to replace my darkness with your light and the joy of Jesus.*

YES, YOU!
. . . one man's act of righteousness leads to justification and life for all (Romans 5:12-19; v. 18).
God says, "You are righteous," and we shrink from this declaration, saying, "Not me." Yes, you! For Christ's sake, God says you are righteous. Something indescribable happens within us when we hear this news. It is entirely different from "I'll try harder" or "I'll make myself into a better person." By the righteousness of Jesus God makes us righteous. We want to help God along in this project, but really, it is God who does it, and the results are entirely different. *Yes, Lord, let it be to me according to your Word.*

INTO CHRIST AND FROM CHRIST
. . . one man's act of righteousness leads to justification and life for all (Romans 5:12-19; v. 18).
Jesus Christ makes us righteous. Jesus Christ makes us alive. Jesus Christ gives us hope and promises life beyond life. Jesus Christ gives us access and peace with God. Jesus Christ enables us to live in the righteousness that he himself gives to us. All things flow into Christ and from Christ. Our purpose is to join the testimony of the apostle and make it our own. *Lord Jesus, you have made me your own; I pray that I may live the righteous life you have made for me.*

IN EVERY TIME OF NEED
'Do not put the Lord your God to the test' (Matthew 4:5-7; v. 7).
In desperation a baby is thrown from a fourth floor window of a burning building and is safely caught by a policeman. Thanks be to God! Unusual circumstances require unusual responses. Normally

behavior that puts our bodies and souls at risk is our responsibility. If we suffer from our foolishness, we can only blame ourselves. Nevertheless, we are to use God's name "in every time of need to call on, pray to, praise and give thanks to God" (from Luther's *Small Catechism*, explanation to the Second Commandment). *Warn me, O God, when I am being foolish.*

BREAD FOR TODAY, AND FOREVER
'One does not live by bread alone' (Matthew 4:1-4; v. 4).
'. . . but by every word that comes from the mouth of God.' When we are hungry we gobble up everything in sight, and still we are not satisfied. Bread is important and God commands us to share our bread with those who have none. But bread is not God, and our hunger is for the God who gives us life and the bread that sustains life. When we still feel empty, what is missing is God. When we are in the wilderness looking for God, it is Jesus who finds us and becomes for us the Bread of Life. *Give us this day our daily bread, and the Bread of Life give us always.*

Nicodemus: Part I
NICODEMUS . . . CAME TO JESUS
[Note: The Greek word *anothen* can mean either 'anew, again,' or 'from above.' Taken together the two meanings give depth to the saying of Jesus.]

BORN ANEW
"*. . . unless one is born anew*" [(RSV) John 3:1-10; v. 3].
Born 'anew' because flesh is flesh and always will be, until its energies are reworked by the Spirit to gain a new identity. In the water of baptism, which is our participation in Christ's death and rising, we gain that new identity, and the Spirit gently breathes in us, giving us the breath of life and making us truly alive. *By your Holy Breath, Lord God, let me become a living being.*

Nicodemus: Part II
BORN FROM ABOVE

"... *no one can see the kingdom of God without being born from above*" (John 3:1-10; v. 3).

"From above" because ultimately salvation—the believing and 'seeing the kingdom'—is God's work, initiated by the Spirit. We need the wind (the Spirit) of God to blow over us and through us, for refreshment, and to instill in us the kind of faith so strong that it is willing to trust God's grace. *Holy Breath of God, refresh my spirit and give me eyes to see your kingdom.*

Nicodemus: Part III
GROWING INTO NEWNESS

"*How can anyone be born after having grown old?*" (John 3:1-8; v. 4).

Young people inspire by their openness to the present and the future. People who have more past than future inspire by their willingness to try new things. Can we grow in Christ after having grown old? Can attitudes be changed, new behaviors learned, even after a lifetime of struggle? The wind, the breath of God, the Holy Spirit, makes it possible even for old Christians to experience newness of life. *O God, I pray for courage to let myself grow into the fullness of Christ my Savior.*

Nicodemus: Part IV
SEEING AND BELIEVING

"... *how can you believe . . . ?*" (John 3:11-15; v. 12).

We are earthlings, and heavenly things are out of our league. Earthly things are still too marvelous for us to fully comprehend. What God has revealed to us on earth is the cross of Christ. This is where we find Christ exalted, lifted up, and it is for our salvation. We have seen the cross, and we can believe that there is even more wisdom and love here than meets the eye. *O Christ, exalted Lord, lifted up on the cross for all to see your dying love: May it be enough to satisfy my needs and doubts.*

Nicodemus: Part V
NOT TO CONDEMN

"... *not to condemn the world* ..." (John 3:16-17; v. 17).

It is not easy to ask the right questions about God. "Where was God in all this?" they ask in the aftermath of tragedy, as though disaster and destruction represent God's message to the world. We must always point to Jesus as God's Word to a world suffering from all manner of tragedy and evil. By his death we can be assured that there is no tragedy where God is not present, suffering and enduring all with his people. By the resurrection of Christ God wills to save the world from every and all evil. In Christ, "God so loved the world . . . not . . . to condemn the world." *I give you praise and thanks, heavenly Father, that you sent Jesus to save me from sin, death and evil.*

SLIPPERY PATHS

He will not let your foot be moved (Psalm 121; v. 3).

The pilgrims went up to God's temple for worship. On their journey they made their way on straight paths and crooked, clambering up one side of the hill and taking care not to go head over heels on the way down. The road may be straight and level, or there may be testings of patience, of love, of faithfulness. The ascents, the ups, are hard enough. The downs, the descents, are often treacherous. God who loves you in Jesus Christ will not let your foot slip. *Gracious God, whose paths are always righteous: My feet are often pointed in the wrong direction. This will explain why I am hanging on to you for Dear Life.*

Sitting by the Well: Part I
IF ONLY THEY KNEW

"*If you knew the gift of God* . . ." (John 4:5-15; v. 10).

There are many who live each day with a burden of guilt that weighs them down and deprives them of the normal joys. If only they knew God's gift of forgiveness in Jesus Christ! There are many estranged from family and friends because of hardness of heart, or misunderstanding, or trauma of some sort. If only they knew the gift of God for reconciliation among enemies! There are many who have positioned themselves far away from God. If only they knew the gift of God! *Do not let me forget your Great Gift, O God, for Jesus' sake.*

Sitting by the Well: Part II
THE RIGHT TOOLS

"Sir, you have no bucket, and the well is deep" (John 4:10-14; v. 11).
We think evangelism is all about technique. If only we had the right bucket! The well is deep, deeper than the Samaritan woman knew, but she was looking at the wrong well. Jesus himself is the well, with grace that is deep enough for all our needs, and the water refreshes and renews like nothing else. If Jesus is the content of our evangelism, the technique will take care of itself. *Lord Jesus, my bucket seems to be empty. Fill it, please, with the grace that I am needing in this moment.*

Sitting by the Well: Part III
A WEARISOME SEARCH

Jesus said to her, "I am he" (John 4:21-26; v. 26).
Looking . . . looking . . . looking . . . sometimes frantically . . . for what is worthwhile and meaningful and above all, lasting. Love, acceptance, forgiveness and victory over sin, death and evil come from God through Jesus Christ. We were weary and we were thirsty. Then we sat down to rest and Jesus asked us for a drink. It is Jesus who has a strong desire to have a relationship with us and to bring us into communion with God. Joining our deepest yearnings with the yearnings of God, Jesus says, "I am he." *I thank you, Lord Jesus, for introducing yourself to me.*

Sitting by the Well: Part IV
FOOD THAT SATISFIES

"I have food to eat that you do not know about" (John 4:27-34; v. 32).
God's grace needs to be communicated to a co-worker troubled by a family situation. A friend has a need that you can't resolve but, by

faith, Jesus can. Close to you, someone is under a cloud. You are there, as though Christ is making himself present to that loved one. The grace of the Lord Jesus is just the medicine for an acquaintance with a heavy conscience. Being the mediator of God's grace is amazingly worthwhile and meaningful, for both ends of the conversation. It is food that satisfies beyond description. *Send me, Lord.*

Sitting by the Well: Part V
OPPORTUNISM

"One sows and another reaps" (John 4:35-38; v. 37).

It is unlikely that a person's faith is the result of only one encounter with one of God's witnesses. Even if there is a conversion event, even if someone brags about 'leading someone to Christ,' it is probable that other circumstances prepared the way. It is a system that keeps us from being too proud of our accomplishments as witnesses and workers in the kingdom. It also points to the importance of every opportunity for sowing the seed, either in word or deed. *Some can say how many they have led to you, Lord Jesus. I would be happy just to say I have sown some seed.*

Sitting by the Well: Part VI
MANY BELIEVED

Many Samaritans . . . believed in him . . . many more believed . . . we believe . . . for ourselves . . . (John 4:39-42).

Faith has many stages along our way to the full stature in Christ. Initially we believe because of someone's example—a parent, a friend, maybe even on the word of a famous person. At some point, however, we come into contact with Jesus Christ himself. There come times when, in the power of the Spirit, we *hear* the gospel, we *know* it is for us, *for me,* and we give up resisting the power of the Lord Jesus to raise us to newness of life. *I have heard your Word, Lord God, and I believe it is for me.*

LOW-TECH COMMUNICATION
O that today you would listen to his voice (Psalm 95; v. 7).
The air is full of communication. First radio waves, then television, now cell phones and WIFIs and what have you. If electronic waves were visible the air would be so thick we couldn't see anything else. Now comes a distinctly low-tech voice, filled with longing to be heard. It is God's voice that can be accessed in the moments of silence that we create or those that present themselves out of nowhere. The voice of God comes in visible wave lengths in Jesus Christ. O that today you would listen his voice! *Heavenly Father, I am trying to be quiet. Still my restlessness, for Jesus's sake.*

March 25
THE ANNUNCIATION OF OUR LORD
Nothing will be impossible for God (Luke 1:26-38; v. 37).
Our first thought is usually to raise objections. There is a plan, a proposal, an idea, but just as quickly there are all kinds of reasons why it should not be considered. Scripture is full of impossible plans—Abraham and Sarah, Hannah, David vs. Goliath, Mary, the Cross! If God chooses to use us, unimpressive as we may be, to be instruments of God's grace, power and love, what can we say except, *"Here am I, the servant of the Lord; let it be with me according to your word."*

Out of Darkness: Part I
DAY LABORERS
"We must work the works of him who sent me while it is day; night is coming when no one can work" (John 9:1-12; v. 4).
Warnings about the limitations of time available usually are directed to people who need a drastic change in their lives. Here the admonition is to people who have already experienced the grace of the Lord Jesus, and whose mission it is to gather others into this fellowship with God. Night is coming when no one can work. While it is day, there are opportunities for our witness. A word unspoken to an

afflicted soul, or a loving deed not done, or an outreach ministry ignored by our congregation will haunt us for a long time. Fortunately, the Holy Spirit's persistence will keep us alert. *Lord Jesus, my tongue seems to be tied at the wrong times. Help me to speak up, in love for your people and in Your Name.*

Out of Darkness: Part II
MUD THERAPY

"He put mud in my eyes" (John 9:13-23; v. 15).

Whether or not Jesus was a practioner of the ancient art of mud therapy, it is intriguing that Jesus covers the man's eyes in order to unveil them. We resist the touch on 'the place where it hurts' but that is where the healing needs to happen. The precious power of Jesus' own saliva mixed with dirt is just exactly what we need, applied to the place in our lives that keeps us in darkness. Then healing takes place in the washing. *Lord Jesus, do not let me be afraid of Your Touch.*

Out of Darkness: Part III
WE ARE NOT OUR OWN

The Lord is my shepherd (Psalm 23; v.1).

When we recite this beloved psalm (from memory?) we might be making a greater claim than we are prepared to embrace. If the Lord is our shepherd, it means we are not in control of our own lives. Sheep that claim a shepherd will relinquish their own will and ideas in order to follow the shepherd in obedience and trust. We surely want the green pastures and still waters. The self-denial and cross, not so much. Nevertheless, it is the Good Shepherd, Jesus Christ, who leads us through the Valley and into Life. *Lord Jesus, you are my shepherd, the One Whom I want.*

Out of Darkness: Part IV
SPIRITUAL INSIGHT
"Though I was blind, now I see" (John 9:24-34; v. 25).
When physical sight is restored all join to praise God. Most of the time, however, this story speaks to us in a spiritual sense. Gaining spiritual insight is no less a miracle than restoration of eyesight. When hardened and stubborn souls give way to the warmth of the Spirit's call it also brings forth unrestrained praise of God. If we can look back on a time of darkness in our own lives and notice how God has brought us into the light of Christ, we pause, as the hymn says, *". . . lost in wonder, love and praise."*

Out of Darkness: Part V
JUDGMENT
"I came into this world for judgment" (John 9:35-41; v. 39).
Here is a slight hiccup in the accepted narrative about Jesus. We thought John the Baptist was the judge and Jesus the kind Shepherd-Savior. The threat from Jesus, however, is only for those who see, or think they see, for the self-satisfied, the know-it-alls. On the other hand , for those who grope blindly, struggling to find their way through life, and who know their lives do not measure up, Jesus is in fact the kind Shepherd who gives His Life for the sheep. *Gracious heavenly Father, I thank you for light and life through Christ my Lord.*

Out of Darkness: Part VI
NO MERE FIGURE OF SPEECH
Once you were darkness, but now in the Lord you are light (Ephesians 5:8-14; v. 8). These arresting words are not a simile, as though we were merely *like* darkness. Without Christ we *were* darkness, spreading gloom and sadness wherever we went. But now we are in Christ, filled with his grace, transformed by his love. So we *are* light, because we are in Christ and Christ is in us. *Such a tremendous transformation, dear God, gives me a strange sensation.*

Out of Darkness: Part VII
REVEALING

. . . in the Lord you are light (Ephesians 5:8-14; v. 8).

There is light from above and light from below. An effective way to enhance the features of a room or a building is with an uplight. The uplight reveals things that are not normally apparent by regular lighting. We are God's uplights. In Christ we *are light*, revealing Christ's light of forgiveness, love, and hope, shining on people around us who do not always get the light. It makes the world a much more interesting place. *Shine, Jesus, through me.*

DRY BONES

O dry bones, hear the word of the Lord (Ezekiel 37:1-6; v. 4).

The word of the Lord is for you when you pray and pray and pray . . . and are still waiting for an answer. It is for you when you are discouraged by your own efforts and disappointed by the actions of others. The word is for you when you feel nothing, when you are neither hot nor cold, but simply dried out. The Word of the Lord is Jesus Christ who is sending his Spirit for your renewal. *Lord God, let your Holy Breath renew my body and soul.*

DEATH

"Lazarus is dead" (John 11:7-16; v. 14).

Jesus tried to soften the blow by using the metaphor of sleep. When the disciples did not catch on he needed to be blunt. When the disciples did not catch on he needed to be blunt. Our friend is dead. Not 'passed on,' or 'passed away.' Not even 'in a better place.' But dead. The heart stopped. No oxygen to the brain. The heat escapes and the flesh is cold and clammy. The body is put away in a grave to cover the stench. Over against this penultimate reality Jesus goes to Bethany to raise the dead! *Almighty God, I praise you for the promise of life eternal, by the resurrection of Jesus.*

Forgiveness

There is forgiveness with you so that you may be feared (Psalm 130: v. 4).
Any ordinary tyrant is feared and by dint of capricious cruelty commands absolute obedience. God exercises His Power chiefly in Showing Mercy. God is sovereign and in control. It is not fear of punishment that ultimately inspires obedience, but forgiveness. We bow low before the Lord our God because he does not keep score of iniquities, but loves, forgives, and renews us for Jesus Christ's sake. *In the depths I praise you, O God.*

We Believe!

"Do you believe . . . ?" (John 11:17-27; v. 26).
In spite of the stone closing the tomb and the stench within, Martha was able to say, "Yes, Lord, I believe." Against the intransigent forces of violence, greed, self-interest and self-promotion; against the intractable foe of death itself; against the sinister workings of evil in our world—empowered by God's Spirit we say, "We believe!" that Jesus Christ is Lord. *Lord, I believe you are the resurrection and the life.*

Unbound

"Unbind him and let him go!" (John 11:38-44; v. 44).
The grave clothes that bind us are old habits and attitudes, low expectations of what God can do, fears of various kinds, eagerness to please ourselves rather than God, self-justification rather than trust in God's grace . . . and the bindings thicken round and round, layer upon layer. "Unbind him!" Jesus says. "Let her go!" *With all my heart I take refuge in Christ . . . who restores me to life.*

The Spirit of Jesus Christ

You are in the Spirit (Romans 8:6-11; v. 9).
Don't waste your time trying to figure out how to "get the Spirit." You have been given the Spirit of God, the Holy Spirit, the Spirit of Jesus Christ. You are in the Spirit! This is God's promise and gift to you,

conveyed through baptism, renewed through the Means of Grace. It is God's Spirit who gives you a thirst for God, and it is God's Spirit who brings you to faith in Christ. *Divine Holy Spirit, increase my faith.*

Monday in Holy Week
THE MIND OF CHRIST

. . . the mind that was in Christ Jesus (Philippians 2:5-11; v. 5).

The human mind is all about power and glory, possessing and keeping, controlling others and pleasing ourselves. The mind of Christ is about yielding, relinquishing legitimate rights and claims, self-offering rather than self-service. The work of Christ's mind is for our benefit, and originates in the love of God. By his obedience and humility we are made righteous children of God.

Heavenly Father, I wish to learn the mind of Christ.

Tuesday in Holy Week
CLINGING TO CHRIST

Who will declare me guilty? (Isaiah 50:4-9; v. 9).

God's law declares us to be guilty. Even if we are not dogged by an aggressive prosecuting attorney, our own conscience will accuse us. In spite of the overwhelming evidence against us, it is the same Lord God who helps us. For Jesus Christ's sake, not even God will condemn us. Therefore, as Katie Luther said as she was nearing death, "I will cling to Christ as a burr clings to an overcoat." *Gracious God, heavenly Father, have mercy on me, for Jesus' sake.*

Wednesday in Holy Week
A SHINING FACE

Let your face shine upon your servant (Psalm 31:9-16; v. 16).

On that gloomy day the cross produced its own radiance. We know that on days when we experience 'the cross' there is no sun, only clouds and ominous rumblings. The cross of Jesus, God's Servant, also stands starkly, lonely, against the background of abandonment. A voice comes from somewhere in our memory, "This is my Son with whom I am well pleased." Whatever beclouds our life, in Christ the face of God shines on us as well. *Lord Jesus, in Your Presence there is fullness of joy* (Psalm 16).

Maundy Thursday
GETTING REAL

"My body . . . my blood . . ." (Matthew 26:17-30; vv. 26, 28).
It doesn't get more real than this, on this side of heaven. In, with, and under the bread and wine of Holy Communion it is Jesus himself who touches us with his grace and power. The wafer stuck to the roof of your mouth or the morsel of bread between our teeth, the wine burning in your stomach—this is Jesus who touches you for forgiveness of sins and for power to live the gospel life. There is nothing symbolic about it. It is really Jesus reaching out from eternity to touch you in time and space. *Lord Jesus, may your Body and your Blood help me to love others as you have loved me.*

Good Friday
FORSAKEN, AND NOT FORSAKEN

"My God, why have your forsaken me?" (Matthew 27:45-46; v 46).
Here is the great mystery that we will never fully understand but which wraps its arms around us and will not let go. The Son of God experienced the pain of utter abandonment. There is now no place, no abyss, no suffering and no sadness where God, in Christ, is not always present. Especially when the question "Why?" goes unanswered, we should know that Jesus Christ is there. The absolute abandonment of Jesus means that there is always absolute love of God for us. *My God, I call to you and am convinced that you hear me, for Jesus Christ's sake.*

The Vigil of Easter
IN AND OUT OF HELL

"Where I am going, you cannot come" (John 13:31-35; v. 33).
Jesus was going into the hell of hatred, suffering, anguish and condemnation, a hell created and imposed by humanity's inhumanity.

We certainly do not want to go there. Jesus sends us, instead, into a new direction, with a new commandment: to love each other as Christ has loved us. Hatred, prejudice, jealousy, and cruel indifference are the very things that create hell on earth. The cross of Jesus frees us to move in the opposite direction. *Praise be to you, Lord God, for victory over sin, death and hell, through Jesus Christ my Lord.*

THE SHROUD OF JERUSALEM

We'd like a cloth, they said, to bury a friend.
The eager linen merchant gravely bowed
And thought how much the customers would spend
To get their friend a worthy linen shroud.
With cloth around the body gently rolled
They lay their friend on borrowed burial bench,
The body now by nature turning cold,
The spice applied against the coming stench.
The tomb is sealed, imperial guard in place;
Behind the stone, all still and dark inside
Until unearthly power rocked that space
And early visitors left mystified.
  Those who closed the tomb had not in mind
  To see the linen shroud was left behind.

III. Easter

If Christ is risen, nothing else matters.
And, if Christ is not risen, nothing else matter.
--Jaroslav Pelikan, 1923-2006

SHAKING THINGS UP
. . . a great Earth Quake (Matthew 28:1-10; v. 2).
The world became topsy-turvy at the dawn of the New Day, the Eighth Day of Creation, the Day of Resurrection, the most glorious of all days, the Lord's Day from now on and forever. Sin's power to corrupt, condemn and control is overthrown in the resurrection of Jesus Christ. Death no longer has the last word. God's first and last word for us is life through Jesus Christ. The resurrection of Jesus sets the whole world trembling. When the dishes stop rattling and the dust settles we see that the world is a very different place indeed. *I'm all shook up, dear God, and grateful.*

THE NAME
". . . everyone who believes in him receives forgiveness of sins through his name" (Acts 10:34-43; v. 43).
When unpleasant memories appear in our consciousness, the cry of "Jesus!" brings relief, because the Name means forgiveness. When we feel the shame of something that we are truly sorry for it is the Name of Jesus that removes the guilt and lifts or countenance. In the same way, when there is someone else's offense that is hard to forgive, it is the Name of Jesus that softens our heart to enable forgiveness. *O*

God, I praise you for the Name of Jesus, in all my needs. Blessed be The Name!

AN ODDLY SHAPED STONE
. . . the stone that the builders rejected . . . (Psalm 118:14-24; v. 22).
The plans of God do not always fit in with our plans, humanly speaking. A builder has a plan. These stones will fit together just so, but here is an oddly shaped Stone, one who ". . . went about doing good and healing all who were oppressed by the devil" (Acts 10:38). The builders do not know what to do with that Stone. They had never dealt with that shape and those dimensions. Out it went, thrown on a rock pile called Calvary. In God's plan this Rejected One is lifted up and made to be the Cornerstone, holding all things together. *"On Christ the solid rock I stand."*

THE OLD NORMAL AND THE NEW REALITY
"Do not be afraid . . . Do not be afraid" (Matthew 28:1-10; vv. 5, 10).
When God intervenes hearts race and flutter and knees are weak. "Do not be afraid," the angel told Bethlehem's shepherds. "Do not be afraid" Jesus said in the middle of a storm. "Do not be afraid" neither of the empty tomb nor at the sight of Jesus. When God approaches the old normal disappears and there is a new reality that affects both hearts and knees. The new reality for us is that Jesus is risen. By his dying and rising he has defeated sin, death and the power of evil for us. *Calm my fears, Lord God, in the Name of the risen Christ.*

A MEETING PLACE
"I have seen the Lord" (John 20:11-18; v. 18).
Mary Magdalene went to the tomb because it was the logical place to find Jesus. It was also the place of her deepest hurt and pain. The resurrection turned the pain into joy and witness. "I have seen the Lord." When we are at the place of deepest pain, despair and need, Jesus meets us there and calls us by name. If you know that the resurrection frees you from the grip of sin, death and the oppression of

evil, then you, too, have seen the Lord. *Gracious God, burst through my fears and give me the joy of witness.*

SERVANTS OF GOD'S PEACE
. . . preaching peace by Jesus Christ (Acts 10:34-43; v. 36).
The Name of Jesus is not honored when it is used as a weapon to threaten people, or as a way of deepening divisions that already exist between people, whether between Christians and people of other religions or even between groups of Christians. Jesus Christ is God's peace for us, and Jesus is God's peace for the world. We are servants of God's peace when we are gracious with those who are different, kind to those who mean us harm, forgiving to those whom we consider enemies. *Make me, too, an instrument of the peace of Christ.*

SOMETHING AT THE DOOR
"Peace be with you . . . Peace be with you" (John 20:19-23; vv. 19, 21).
There is something knocking at the door. It may not be the fear of someone coming to arrest us because we are followers of Jesus, but it could be the fear of bills to pay, fear of an undiagnosed symptom, an issue with a family member or some low grade nagging anxiety. If it is a guilty conscience, or a rebellious spirit, or an unwillingness to take up the cross, or a desire to be around but not too close to Jesus—Jesus' word for us is "Peace be with you." *Please, won't you come in, Lord Jesus?*

THE JOY WILL COME
. . . you . . . rejoice with an indescribable and glorious joy (1 Peter 1:3-9; v. 8).
Chancel banners notwithstanding, sometimes Christians just do not feel the joy that seems to bubble up and overflow in some believers. The important thing, however, is not the joy but the faith, which produces the joy. When one responds in faith to God's love for us in Jesus Christ, the joy will come. Think on Jesus, his love, his grace, the gift of second chances, the promise of an imperishable inheritance, and

sooner or later the joy will be there. *Holy Spirit, enable me to experience the joy of the early believers.*

IN THE PRESENCE
In your presence there is fullness of joy (Psalm 16; v. 11).
We don't necessarily need to see Jesus in order to be in his Presence. Only extremely lazy Christians cannot imagine a Presence, unseen, but nevertheless sensed and felt. When we pray we are in God's presence. When we sing or whistle a hymn or spiritual song, or when we encounter someone who is needy, we are in Jesus' Presence. When there is contact with a Christian brother or sister, Jesus is there. In these moments, nothing is lacking, and there is fullness of joy. *Lord Jesus, I know you are Present.*

NOT NORMAL
. . . a new birth . . . (1 Peter 1:3-9; v. 3).
Nicodemus was the first to wonder what a new birth could mean. If we are satisfied with our lives and everything seems normal and safely on the tracks we also might question the need for a new start. It is just exactly because everything seems normal that the new birth is necessary. "Normal" means we have grown accustomed to the rule of sin and death in this world. A new birth, God's gift to us though baptism into Christ Jesus, means sin is defeated in our lives, too, and that life, not death, is God's first and last word for us. *Thanks and praise to you, gracious God, for the new birth in Christ.*

HEAVEN
. . . an inheritance that is imperishable . . . (1 Peter 1:3-9; v. 4).
To think from time to time about heaven is by no means to despise our life on earth. To think about the imperishable inheritance is to think of God who, above all things, loves us. We value this life, and we thank God every day for all the joys and pleasures that this world affords, and we desire these gifts for all. More than that, we assume responsibility to care for the earth to safeguard its good things for

generations to come. And when our work is done, we look for life with God who loves us eternally. *Heavenly Father, I praise you for your love that ever ends.*

Witnessing Thomas
Thomas answered him, "My Lord and my God!" (John 20:19-31; v. 28).
Doubt and faith are really closer together than we often think. People who claim to be doubters are often believers just waiting for an excuse to commit themselves. The amazing thing about Thomas is that he is held up as a 'doubter,' and yet his confession of faith is a ringing affirmation of who Jesus is. He is our Lord and God, and it often takes a doubter to point this out to us. *My Lord and my God, support me in my doubts and in my faith.*

> *Faith is either a struggle or it is nothing.*
> --Helmut Thielicke (1908-1986)

Even If
In this you rejoice, even if . . . (1 Peter 1:3-9; v. 6)
The 'even if' is the hard part. If only the whole world could be gathered up in Easter joy and put aside every difference and motive for divisions and embrace God's reconciliation through Jesus Christ! We who have died with Christ and been raised with him to newness of life know we will "suffer various trials." The baptized will disdain the suffering for the sake of the joy of God's new creation in Jesus Christ. *In my 'various trials,' dear God, keep me focused on your New Creation.*

Keeping the Faith
I kept my faith, even when I said, "I am greatly afflicted" (Psalm 116; v. 10).
Faith's object is God, who is revealed in Jesus Christ as the God who loves, forgives, and keeps us going, come what may. "I kept my faith" is not a boast in oneself, but a boast in God who pulls us through every affliction. The Exodus was a sign of it; our baptism is a

sign, and the resurrection of Jesus is the promise that God's intention is to deliver us from every affliction. *Father in heaven, you are the keeper of my faith.*

Emmaus: Part I
SEEING, AND SEEING

... but their eyes were kept from recognizing him (Luke 24:13-35; v. 16).

A person walks around the house looking for his glasses and finds them on his nose. The obvious is not always obvious until we see it. The risen Christ and the glories of the resurrection are there for all to see, but we need the Spirit to point it all out for us. New attitudes, healthy behaviors, renewed relationships—no one learns these things all at once, and everyone is growing into Christ. Sometimes it is necessary not to be able to 'see' in order for us to come to the place where we can say, "Now I see!" *Lord Jesus, teach me what I need to live the new life today.*

Emmaus: Part II
ASTOUNDED

"... *some women of our group astounded us*" (Luke 24:13-35; v. 22).

Even today there are disciples of Jesus who walk along in deep disappointment, overcome by cynicism, frustrated by hopes and plans that do not turn out as expected. Sometimes the relentless predictability of day to day existence dulls our sensibility to God's presence and power. Prepare to be astounded, again and again! There is a pulse of energy at large in the world. It is the resurrection of Jesus Christ. *Yes, Lord, I am ready to be surprised and even a bit frightened by your resurrection.*

Emmaus: Part III
THE NECESSARY

"*Was it not necessary that the Messiah should suffer these things and enter into his glory?*" (Luke 24:13-27; v. 26).

The redemption of the world was no easy matter. It required the Son of God to humble himself to become not only a human being, but a human suffering servant. Through his suffering he gained the victory and the glory for us. Those who follow Christ should know that the way of discipleship is the way of the cross, and suffering always precedes glory. *Spirit of God, give me courage to say "thy will, not mine, be done" with sincerity.*

Emmaus: Part IV
HOSPITALITY

"Stay with us, because it is almost evening, and the day is now nearly over" (Luke 24:28-35; v. 29).

The two invited Jesus to stay with them before they knew who their Guest was. The glory of hospitality is that when we attend to the needs of others there is blessing for us beyond our expectations. *Thank you, gracious God, for hospitality received.*

Emmaus: Part V
RECOGNITION

"Were not our hearts burning within us . . .?" (Luke 24:28-35; v. 32).

Peering through a microscope the student says to the teacher, "Tell me what I am supposed to be looking at here." Part of the reason we don't 'see' is because we need to be taught. There is no point in opening up the Bible if we think we know it all already. There is no point in listening to a sermon unless we believe God will, somehow, teach us something about Christ. When the Word speaks to us, the Unrecognized One becomes the Revealed One and our hearts burn with that bright, glad flame of understanding. *Spirit of God, grant that I may be teachable.*

The Good Shepherd: Part I
LEARNING NAMES

"He calls his own sheep by name . . . (John 10:1-10; v. 3).

The first step in establishing a relationship is to learn the name. Jesus has broken the ice and calls us by name, even while our back was turned. Day by day and throughout every day, the Good Shepherd calls our name: directing us to the tasks that await us, guiding us in the process of making decisions, and making himself present in the scheduled as well as the chance meetings with people so that the totality of our lives is governed by our relationship with Jesus Christ. *Yes, Lord Jesus, and I know your Name as well.*

The Good Shepherd: Part II
ABUNDANCE

"I came that they may have life, and have it abundantly" (John 10:1-10; v. 10).

The Servant is up early and goes to bed late, after the lords and ladies of the household have their needs attended to. Jesus is our Lord and Master and Sovereign who is also the Chief Servant of the World. He pours himself out, gives his life and body and blood for the sake of a world needing redemption from sin and evil. The abundant life Jesus promises is his own life, the life of the Son of God. This life is righteousness and a profound trust that God will give us everything we need. *Your grace is always sufficient, Lord God.*

The Good Shepherd: Part III
THE RIGHT PATH

He leads me in right paths . . . (Psalm 23; v. 3).

"Making bad decisions" has come to be a euphemism for sinful behavior. A "bad decision" means we have taken the wrong path. Decisions are sometimes reached quickly, impulsively, and sometimes only after prolonged pondering and agonizing. Whether quickly or ponderously, what matters is the leadership of the Lord Jesus Christ. If it is the Lord who is leading us, the path will be the right one. *When I pray for advice, dear God, keep me honest, sincere, and truly open to your leading.*

The Good Shepherd: Part IV
THE GATE GOES IN AND OUT
"I am the gate . . . I am the gate . . ." (John 10:1-10; vv. 7, 9).
Forget about the propaganda of materialism. The gateway into the abundant life is Jesus Christ. Through Jesus we have fellowship with God the Father in the power of the Spirit. Peace and joy and love cannot be gotten in any other way—and it's free. Jesus is also the gateway out, and he leads us to meet the world—our neighbor, co-workers, fellow student, family members—to embody the grace of the Lord Jesus. Our ministry in daily life is to share the abundant life. *May I be a messenger of peace and joy and love, in Jesus' Name.*

The Good Shepherd: Part V
YOU ARE MINE
"He calls his own sheep by name" (John 10:1-10; v. 3).
In a crowd of strangers it is a joy and a relief to find someone who knows your name. In the turmoil and uncertainty of each day's activities, there is one voice that quiets the restless din in our soul. It is the voice of the Good Shepherd who calls us in and leads us out. "Do not fear . . . I have called you by name. You are mine" (Isaiah 43:1). *In so many different daily encounters, may I be the voice of Jesus.*

APOSTOLIC FELLOWSHIP
They devoted themselves to the apostles' teaching and fellowship, to the breaking of bread and the prayers (Acts 2:42-47; v. 47).
Three thousand were added (v. 41) and the life of Christians was characterized by this summary verse. Evangelism and church growth is not a matter of technique or mechanics. Each group of Christians has a unique array of gifts that the Spirit will use for the sake of the gospel of Jesus Christ. We put ourselves in a position to be used mightily by God when we pay attention to "the apostles' teaching and fellowship, the breaking of bread and the prayers." *Come, Holy Spirit, into my fellowship of believers.*

Waiting for the Lord's Day

TIMES AND PLACES
. . . to this you have been called (1 Peter 2:19-25; v. 21).

Discipleship will lead us into times and places where suffering is unavoidable. In response shall we take the sword and cut off someone's ear? We follow instead in the footsteps of Jesus who did not return abuse for abuse nor did he threaten when suffering unjustly. By refusing to return evil for evil he has won the victory. He has freed us from the overpowering urge to bring vengeance on our enemies and by his cross has given us the confidence to trust that God will bend all things according to his plan and purpose. *Free me, dear God, from overpowering urges that interfere with my discipleship.*

April 25
SAINT MARK, EVANGELIST
How beautiful upon the mountains are the feet of the messenger who announces peace, who brings good news (Isaiah 52:7-10; v. 7).

Mark, the one symbolized by a lion, the messenger "who brings good news," is out with the first edition of The Gospel story. He tells the story of Jesus with an urgency worthy of the message. "Immediately" this and "straightway" that, he writes. It is a challenge to Caesar and the powers that be and comfort for all needing redemption. Sing a song of Easter victory on this day. The good news of Jesus Christ, the Son of God, has begun! (Cf. Mark 1:1). *Let your blessing rest, dear God, on all who tell the story of Jesus.*

---

*Philip and James the Younger are remembered on the same day because, according to tradition, their relics arrived in Rome on the same day.

May 1
SAINT PHILIP AND SAINT JAMES, APOSTLES
"Have I been with you all this time, Philip, and you still do not know me?" (John 14:8-14; v. 9).

Presumably, James the Younger was standing nearby when Philip posed his question.* No one wants to be the one who asks a dumb question. Dumb questions are often useful, however, because sometimes even the obvious needs to be pointed out to us. In this case, if Philip hadn't asked we would have to. Show me the Father, Lord Jesus. Show us God! More evidence, please! Look to Jesus and you will see God. Look to Jesus and you will know that God has taken the suffering of the world, sin and even death, into himself, and gives us forgiveness, life, and salvation. This is God's great work in Jesus Christ, and those who believe in Jesus do even greater things (v. 12). *As Christ glorified the Father, I pray that my life may give glory to the Son.*

The Way, the Truth, and the Life: Part I
A WAY OF LIFE

"I am the WAY . . ." (John 14:1-7; v. 6).
Jesus is "the Way" to the Father. Jesus is also our "way of life." We are mistaken if we expect God to bless *our* way of life, or life style. Instead, as Christians, our desire is to conform our lives to the way of Jesus, which means seeking to love God above all else, and our neighbor as ourselves. *In life, witness and service, help me not to lose my Way.*

The Way, the Truth and the Life: Part II
A PERSON

"I am . . . the TRUTH . . ." (John 14:1-7; v. 6).
"What is Truth?" asked Pilate, as though Jesus were a Greek philosopher. Truth is not an abstraction, but a person. It is the reality lived by Jesus Christ. His life was free of pretension and posturing; free from hypocrisy and double standards; free from ambition and greed; free to love and forgive, to heal and restore. Jesus shows us what life is Truly about. *May your Truth find concrete reality in my life, Lord Jesus.*

The Way, the Truth and the Life: Part III
THE BEGINNING, AND THE BEGINNING

"I am . . . the LIFE . . ." (John 14:1-7; v. 6).

Jesus is the resurrection and the life. In him we are promised that death is not the end, but the beginning of joy in the presence of God. Jesus is also Life for us now already. We have looked for joy and pleasure and personal fulfillment in places that only prove to be dead ends. Knowing Christ is our joy and pleasure and the fullness of life itself. *Only you make me alive, Lord God.*

ROCK CONCERT

. . . a living stone . . . living stones . . . a cornerstone . . . the stone . . . rejected . . . a stone that makes them stumble (1 Peter 2:2-10; vv. 4ff.).

Peter "the Rock" stages the original rock concert. The images will make us all stumble until we regain our balance by coming to terms with what God has done in Jesus Christ. A stone is not alive, unless it is Jesus Christ, risen from the dead. This living stone offers himself as the cornerstone of a new structure, a new mode of existence. Then he gathers other stones, lifeless, hard, with rough edges, and binds them to himself and they, too, come alive. Those who prefer lifelessness, will stub their toes in this Rock. *Gracious God, by your Spirit align my life with the Life within me, Jesus Christ my Lord.*

LETTING GO

Into your hand I commit my spirit (Psalm 31:1-5; v. 5).

"Let go, and let God," they say in Twelve-step recovery groups. There is a victory that only God can win and it is a victory that comes only when we give up and rest ourselves in God's promises and grace. They mocked Jesus by saying, "Let God deliver him now" (Matthew 27:43). The resurrection was the victory that only God could win. Against attackers, injustice, misfortune, we say "Into your hand I commit my spirit." *Gracious and powerful God, I prayer for faith to trust you for the victory.*

Greater Works?
". . . greater works than these . . ." (John 14:8-14; v. 12).

This is the third rail of Christian discipleship, the one we are afraid to touch. What does Jesus mean by "greater works"? Is he thinking of miracles? Or acts of sublime self-sacrifice? Or calling other people into the life of discipleship? We simply cannot imagine the greater things Jesus has in mind for us. Let us pray that we will be open to however God's power might be manifested in our lives as disciples of Jesus. *Heavenly Father, I am not sure I really want such power. Remove my fears and make me ready for whatever tasks you call to me to do.*

A Strange Place
. . . like living stones, let yourselves be built into a spiritual house (1 Peter 2:2-10; v. 5).

Stones that move, breathe, grow and change shape! The world Christians inhabit is a strange place indeed. We are governed by a power originating in the death and resurrection of Jesus Christ. Our hardness is transformed by grace. Joined to Christ the cornerstone, we are built into a house where love and joy give welcome to other stones hardened by the experiences of life. *Gracious God, heavenly Father, let this stone come alive to grow into the shape of Jesus Christ.*

Evangelizing with Paul: Part I
Athens
I . . . looked carefully at the objects of your worship . . . (Acts 17:22-31: v. 23).

Strolling through Athens it was not hard for the Apostle Paul to discern the objects of the Athenians' affections. A stranger might pass through our neighborhoods and streets and homes and discover the things we are passionate about. To Athenians of all ages looking for something but not knowing what, Paul announces the God "not made with human hands" but the God who became human, in whom "we live and move and have our being." *Show me the objects of my worship, Lord.*

Evangelizing with Paul: Part II
FINDING THE UNKNOWN GOD

'To an unknown god' (Acts 17:22-31; v. 23).

The gods of the Greeks had familiar names, but to cover all the bases the Athenians had even erected an alar to 'an unknown god.' The 'unknown god' that Paul made known to the Athenians was the God revealed in the death and resurrection of Jesus Christ. Even though we do not worship idols of metal or stone, perhaps we will manage to fool ourselves about the presence of 'other gods' in our lives. Unknown to us, perhaps, or unrecognized, but still holding power over us. Luther wrote, "Anything on which you heart relies and depends, I say, that is really your God" (--Martin Luther, *Large Catechism*). Scrolling through our attitudes and behaviors we will see just exactly what, or who, has center stage in our life. *God and Lord, in whom we 'live and move and have our being,' release my grip from the things that keep me from loving you above all things.*

Evangelizing with Paul: Part III
NATIONALISM

From one ancestor he made all nations . . . (Acts 17:22-31; v. 26).

Everyone is by nature partial to their own place of birth. There are often feelings of superiority in relation to other countries, and sometimes there are feelings of jealousy when others cross our borders. We should caution ourselves about extreme nationalism, however. If all nations come from one ancestor, we are all related to each other, and all are God's children. We know that God confers no "most favored nation" status on anyone, but loves us all dearly and deeply in Jesus Christ. *Increase my love for you, and for my neighbor as well.*

Evangelizing with Paul: Part IV
THE FREE GIFT

God . . . now commands all people everywhere to repent (Acts 17:22-31; v. 30).

All people everywhere—from wicked terrorists to pious churchly people—are intent on sanctifying their own way of life and making their own point of view the standard by which everyone else is to be judged. All fall short of God's glory, however, and all need God's free gift of forgiveness through Jesus Christ. The free gift is not culturally conditioned, nor should it be confused with religious dominance. It is mediated through the love of Christian people who know how to forgive just as they have been forgiven. *Gracious God, do not let my arrogance stand in the way of reconciliation with you or with anyone else; in Jesus' Name.*

Although you have not seen him, you love him; and even though you do not see him now, you believe in him and rejoice with an indescribable and glorious joy. (1 Peter 1:8)

ASCENSION DAY

They were continually in the temple blessing God (Luke 24:44-53).

Disappeared from sight! Still, they were not deterred from blessing God. The Ascension means Jesus is Lord of heaven and earth, redeemer from sin, conqueror of death and all evil powers. Our Lord rules by grace in the hearts and minds of all who will believe his story. *Lord God, fill me with the glorious joy of believing; in Jesus' Name.*

INTO GLORY

"I will not leave you orphaned" (John 14:15-21; v. 18).

The Ascension of Jesus could have been a double trauma for the disciples. The hope and joy and force of conviction generated by the visible Presence of the risen Lord Jesus could easily have been undercut by his Disappearance into Glory. The One who was mysteriously present suddenly and more mysteriously was visible no longer. We are not orphans, however. In the power of the Holy Spirit Jesus is with us in Word and Sacrament. "In with and under" the bread and wine we are assured of his Presence. *Lord Jesus, though I cannot see you, I believe that you are with me with grace and power for all my needs.*

FREED FROM THE MEMORIES
Come and hear . . . and I will tell what he has done for me (Psalm 66).
The story of our conversion may not be so dramatic that we could take it on tour. The psalmist is a more willing witness than most of us would dare to be. The areas of our lives transformed by God's grace may be too personal, too embarrassing to talk about. It may be enough to say that God's grace frees me from the memory of past sins and that forgiveness always means joyful fellowship with God and healthy relationships with my neighbor. *God, leaving painful memories behind, grant me grace to press forward to newness in Christ.*

May 14
SAINT MATTHIAS, APOSTLE
And they put forward two, Joseph called Barsabbas, who was also called Justus, and Matthias (Acts 1:15-26; v. 23).
They felt the need to replace Judas among the apostles. There were two candidates. One with biographical information like that informing voters at a church convention. Joseph, surnamed Barsabbas (possibly meaning 'Son of the Sabbath' in Aramaic). He was also called Justus. What a splendid Christian he must have been! The other candidate is simply named Matthias. We learn his name, and nothing else. They prayed, and the lot fell to Matthias. Then he disappears from the New Testament and from history. That is the story of most Christians. We are called by the Spirit to faith in Christ; we strive to live and serve faithfully; and there are no stained glass windows with our names on

them. Our names are written in the Book of Life, and it is enough. *Dear God, help me to serve faithfully and joyfully in anonymity.*

AN OFFENSE TO THE MIND
"I have made your name known" (John 17:1-11; v. 6).
Here we glimpse the mystery of the Holy Trinity. The Father and the Son have their own identities, and yet they are bound in such a way that One is in the Other and the Other is in the One. It offends the mind but comforts the soul to know that Jesus reveals exactly as much of God as we need to know. What we see is a God of love to Whom we belong, held forever in the Spirit's embrace of the Father and the Son. *Holy and Blessed Trinity, One God now and forever, I give you thanks and praise for your glory revealed in Jesus Christ. Let it be enough for me, for now.*

JESUS IS COMING
"This Jesus . . . will come . . ." (Acts 1:6-14; v. 11).
Wacky interpreters of Scripture make it easy for skeptics and non-believers to hold features of Christian belief up to scorn and ridicule. God's promise is that Christ will return. More than that we cannot say. If the first appearance of Jesus was surrounded by events that could not have been predicted, we can assume that the coming of our Lord Jesus Christ will likewise occur in a form that no one, not even the most bizarre speculators, could imagine. Christ has died. Christ is risen. Christ will come again. *Even so, come, Lord Jesus!*

THE WICKED
. . . as wax melts . . . (Psalm 68:1-10; v. 2).
Some psalms have ideas that are somewhat awkward. On the one hand, we resonate with the wish of the psalmist who imagines the wicked melting away like wax on a burning candle. On the other hand, Christian charity compels us to love, forgive, and pray for those who trouble us. In our conflicted state we turn to the cross, where

Jesus' life melts away, taking with it the sin of the world, making reconciliation of enemies one of the gospel's surprising possibilities. *O God, sometimes I wish some people would just melt away. Give me a warm heart for my enemies, for Jesus Christ's sake.*

ANXIETIES

Cast all your anxieties on him, because he cares for you (1 Peter 5:6-11; v. 7).

"Count your blessings," we sometimes say, as an antidote to difficulty. It's always a good idea to count one's blessings, but here the Apostles invites us to count our anxieties! Make a list of all the things that cause you to worry and lose sleep over, and then give the list to God. God, of course, already knows, but he wants the list from us in any case, so that we may know that these things will be taken care of, for "God cares for us." Then we trust the promise and sleep soundly. *Most gracious heavenly Father, I give you my worrisome attitude in exchange for a trusting spirit; in Jesus' Name.*

DISCIPLINE

Discipline yourselves (1 Peter 5:6-11; v. 8).

"Discipline" (not to be confused with "law") is the self-imposed lifestyle of a Christian disciple for the sake of appropriating the freedom from sin, death and evil that Christ gives us. Reading Scripture, praying whether you feel like it or not, listening for the voice of God to emerge from the stillness, are examples of Christian discipline. Speaking kindly, doing favors, 'going the extra mile,' show discipline as well. And there are even 'greater works' in God's plan. The result of discipline is that our thoughts, our plans and our actions all reflect the power of God at work in us. *Stir me from laziness, fear and despondency, O God, that I may embody discipleship.*

May 31
The Visitation
"And blessed is she who believed that there would be a fulfillment of what was spoken to her by the Lord" (Luke 1:39-57; v. 45).

Mary, full of grace, surprised to be the bearer of God into the world, visits her kinswoman Elizabeth, likewise surprised to be a mother "at her age!" They had much to talk about. Christians likewise, have much to talk about. In a world where there is so much evidence of sin and death, Christians have a message of forgiveness and life through Jesus Christ. Of course we will not know what to say until we have looked into our own lives to see what God has done for us. *My soul magnifies the Lord, and my spirit rejoices in God my Savior* (v. 47).

Prayer
All these were constantly devoting themselves to prayer (Acts 1:6-14; v. 14).

Some names are familiar: Peter and John; Mary, the Lord's mother. Even Simon the Zealot was praying constantly! What keeps us from adding our names to the list of those who were "constantly devoting themselves to prayer"? Without knowing the impending Gift they felt a stirring in their hearts that gave them a strong desire for fellowship with God. If we pay attention, we will discover those same stirrings in our hearts. *Heavenly Father, my spirit wants to pray; the flesh is lazy. Stir me up, by your Spirit; in Jesus' Name.*

IV. Pentecost

THE GIFT

About a hundred twenty, more or less,
Together, drawn by those who said they'd seen
Their Lord alive; they ask what could it mean?
Quite unaware the gift they would possess.
The promised Sprit came in midst of flames
Enabling witness; just as they'd been told.
The Power from on High had made them bold
To say the Name above all other names.
The talk then turns to gifts of Holy Ghost;
Afraid, not sure of what could be in store,
When Holiness is near, some close the door;
Yet who will stand against God's Pentecost?
   No need dismiss exotic gifts so swift,
   It's faith in Christ the Sprit's primary gift.

THIRSTY FOR GOD

"Let anyone who is thirsty come to me" (John 7:37-39; v. 37).

Jesus invites the thirsty. They were thirsty for something but didn't know what. They came to Jesus and discovered they were thirsty for God. They were thirsty for a day without the nagging thoughts of guilt. They were thirsty to be free of resentment, anger, the desire for more and more. They were thirsty for the knowledge that they could walk away from their compulsions. Jesus calls (cries out!) to those who are thirsty. *I thirst.*

WATER
"Out of the believer's heart shall flow rivers of living water" (John 7:37-39; v. 38).
Jesus is the source of the living water, but the water (Spirit) flows in and overflows the inner being of those who believe in Jesus. The life that Jesus gives is imparted to us through the Spirit. It not only gives us life but overflows so that those around us are also blessed. *Come, Holy Spirit!*

GRUESOME WOUNDS
. . . he showed them his hands and his side (John 20:19-23;v. 20).
The gruesome side of the resurrection reminds us of how it all came about. We know it is Jesus because of the wounds. The Risen Lord is also the Crucified One. The one who bears the wounds lives and by his wounds our sins are forgiven, broken hearts are healed, and our relationship with God and those whom God loves is fully restored. In spite of the wounds we bear in body or soul, God's word to us in Jesus Christ is life. *Lord Jesus, by your resurrection power heal the deep wounds of body or soul that have scarred my life, that I may live forever in newness of life.*

THE BODY
. . . he breathed on them . . . (John 20:19-23; v. 22).
The spiritual cannot do without the physical. God wants our bodies. Just as God filled the first human with the life-giving Breath, so the Lord Jesus breathes His Spirit into our nostrils and makes us alive. We need that breath, that oxygen, that Spirit, so that our bodies have energy for the Christian life. It is with our bodies that we lift hands

and voice to God in prayer and praise; it is with our bodies that we "do unto others" as God has done for us. It is in our bodies that Christ, through His Spirit, dwells. *When your Spirit breathes, Lord God, I feel full of life.*

A Refreshing Breeze

When you send forth your spirit they are created . . . renew . . . (Psalm 104:24-35; v. 30).

There is a time for creation and a time for renewal. When things are beyond repair, the Spirit of God again and again broods over the chaos. God's word (Jesus) speaks and there is a new creation. When we are weary and tired out, there comes a refreshing breeze. It is God breathing the grace of Jesus Christ to renew exhausted sols. We never look in vain for the sending of the Spirit, who embraces the universe and always responds to our needs. *Holy Spirit, I lift my hands as though hosting a sail, and I wait.*

A Different Kind of Wine

"They are filled with new wine" (Acts 2:1-21; v. 13).

They were indeed filled with new wine, but not the kind the scoffers had in mind. They were filled with the new wine of the Holy Spirit, empowering them to do wonderful things in the name of Jesus Christ. The wine that comes in a bottle lowers inhibitions and people who drink too much of it might do things they otherwise wouldn't do. The new wine that comes from the Holy Spirit also enables us to do things we wouldn't dare to do on our own. The Spirit frees us to be bold and daring for God. *Holy Spirit, fill me with that new wine of the power from on high; for Jesus' sake.*

JESUS IS LORD
No one can say 'Jesus is Lord' except by the Holy Spirit (1 Corinthians 12:3-13; v. 3).
Praise God! We have the gift of the Spirit. The proof is our confession that Jesus Christ is Lord. It is the same Spirit who gives us courage to open our minds and hearts (and maybe even to raise our arms; or maybe not!) to new impulses and new directions of life and service in Jesus' name. The same Spirit allows us to be captured by the grace of God, comforted in affliction, and emboldened in witness. *Lord Jesus, how joyful it is to name you as my Lord.*

THE HOLY TRINITY
The grace of the Lord Jesus Christ, the love of God, and the communion of the Holy Spirit be with all of you (2 Corinthians 13:1-13; v 13).
The context of our lives, the environment we live in, the air we breathe, are all imbued with the grace, love, and companionship of God. Our mission is to involve more and more people in this Trinitarian fellowship. *If your grace, love and companionship are "in me," I need nothing else.*

GOD'S SELF-DISCLOSURE
. . . *grace* . . . *love* . . . *communion* [koinonia: *fellowship, sharing*] (2 Corinthians 13:1-13; v. 13).
The Holy Trinity (One in Three; Three in One) is a mystery that defies logical explanation. Every analogy will break down sooner or later. It is, however, a mystery to be meditated on, considered, discussed, and above all, believed. God's self-disclosure to a world broken and divided by sin and evil wraps us up in grace and love and opens us to the heart of God. *Lord God, mysterious and majestic, I thank you for grace, love, and your fellowship in my life.*

THOSE DOUBTERS
Some doubted (Matthew 28:16-20; v. 17).
It seems dubious to us that they could doubt what their own eyes were telling them. Jesus Christ, whom they had seen crucified, was very much alive, standing right before them. We might want to grab those doubters and shake them into belief. Jesus, however, is not perturbed. He commands all his disciples, whether they are fervent believers or tepid doubters, to "Go, make disciples." Those who bend to the authority of Jesus will find their faith. *Gracious God, I, too, sometimes find myself among the doubters. Above the chatter of the naysayers, let me hear the clear command of Christ.*

MAKING DISCIPLES
Baptizing . . . teaching . . . (Matthew 28:16-20; vv. 19, 20).
The coin of making disciples has two sides, each one dependent on the other for content and purpose. We *baptize* because this is where we are physically connected, by water and word, to the death and resurrection of Christ. Baptism is where our life in Christ begins and draws its energy. We *teach*, and the content of our teaching is what God has done in Jesus Christ and made real for us through Holy Baptism. *Father, Son, and Holy Spirit, today I remember that I have been baptized. Help me to walk in newness of life.*

THE HOLY NAME OF GOD
. . . how majestic is your name (Psalm 8; v. 1).
So majestic, in fact, the psalmist, or at least those reading or chanting the psalm would have substituted the holy Name *Yahweh* for the generic 'LORD.' The God revealed to Moses as 'I AM WHO I AM' now is revealed as 'Father, Son, and Holy Spirit.' There is mystery and incomprehensibility in the idea of triunity: one in three and three in one. That is the way it should be. It is far better that God understands us than that we should understand God. A god fully knowable and understandable is a god with no majesty at all. The majestic greatness

of our God is seen chiefly in the suffering, death and resurrection of the Son, Jesus Christ our Lord. *Holy God, I am here, before You, in awe and reverence.*

THIS COMPLICATED NAME
"In the name of the Father, and of the Son, and of the Holy Spirit" (Matthew 28:16-20; v. 19).

We were baptized into this complicated Name. This is our joy and comfort. We are taken up into the majesty of the Triune God, into the care of the God who made all things good; carried into the new creation by God's Son; sustained always by the Spirit who sees our every need and who breathes the life of God into us. When we hear the phrase, "In the name of . . ." it rings a bell. It was the first blessing we heard at baptism, and the source of every blessing from then on. *Gracious God, majestic beyond all knowing, yet you have made yourself known in your Son Jesus in the power of the Spirit; I believe that you have joined your Name to mine, in baptism.*

WHEN THINGS ARE FINE
"I am with you always" (Matthew 28:16-20; v. 20).

The Lord did not say that everything will be fine all the time. He simply says, "I am with you always." When things are fine we can almost feel the presence of Jesus, unless we are distracted by the "fineness" of the moment. When things are tough, we still have the promise. When things are not fine, the cross is the sign that Jesus is with us. The One who promises to be with us always is the resurrected Lord, the conqueror. Then, even when we are not "fine," we are fine. *Thank you, Lord Jesus, for the promise. Help me to remember it, even when things are fine.*

June 11
SAINT BARNABAS, APOSTLE
. . . he exhorted them all to remain faithful to the Lord with steadfast devotion (Acts 11:19-30; v. 23).

Generous, donating a piece of land to the church (Acts 4:37); and open to receiving Gentiles into the faith (11:23), as well as that former archenemy Saul

(9:27), Barnabas was the kind of gracious servant of God without which the church becomes rigid and impervious to the Spirit of God. During worship at Antioch, the Spirit said, "Set apart for me Barnabas and Saul for the work to which I have called them." Barnabas and Saul set out on what is called [Paul's] first missionary journey. Simeon, Lucius and Manaen (13:1) stayed behind in Antioch. The Lord had other work them, and for us, too. In worship we listen to the Spirit to discern what God is calling us to do. *Bless us, O Lord, with the graciousness of your servant Barnabas.*

A Silent Witness

Write them on the doorposts of your house . . . (Deuteronomy 11:18-21; v. 20).

Some people have favorite Bible verses hanging on the wall in their home, or maybe on a refrigerator magnet, or taped to a computer monitor. The plaque affixed to the front door of one home quoted Joshua 24:15: "As for me and my household . . ." It was a silent witness to the mail carrier, the newspaper delivery person, and to all guests. Even the occupants of the house were reminded of their own witness every time they came home. *Your word is a lamp to my feet.*

Power

The gospel . . . is the power of God . . . (Romans 1:16-17; v. 16).

The gospel—the word that means God justifies sinners for Jesus Christ's sake—has turned the world upside down more than once and continues to do so in our own lives as well. Souls have responded in faith, hope and love to the proclamation of the grace of God. The usual symbols of power—sword and spear—coerce compliance but do not transform human life. Signs of God's New Creation appear where sinners experience forgiveness and enemies start to pray for each other. *I need the power of the Good News every day, Lord God.*

God's Will

. . . the one who does the will of my Father in heaven (Matthew 7:21-29; v. 21).

There is a fascination with "deeds of power," whether by machines of war or by spiritual practices. We would all like to know the secret word that results in prodigious signs and wonders. The deeds Jesus has been talking about are the deeds of peacemaking, of turning the other cheek, of hiding one's piety instead of showing it off. The "will of my Father" will lead us, like Jesus, to the cross. This is where God's power will be revealed, for Jesus, and for us as well. *Thy will be done also in my life, heavenly Father.*

Weather Aware

The rain fell . . . the winds blew . . . (Matthew 7:21-29; vv. 25, 27).

The life built on the vicissitudes of fortune is precarious indeed. Wealth accumulates and dissipates with every change of wind. "Let the good times roll" because we know they will not last forever. At some point there will be a final illness or event that will test the foundation of our lives. The solid foundation is the life of discipleship, taking the yoke of Jesus (Matthew 11:29) and making it one's own. *Lord God, when the winds blow, I will steady myself by trusting you; in Jesus' Name.*

A Mighty Fortress

You are indeed my rock and my fortress (Psalm 31; v. 3).

We Christians, following the example of Jesus, strive to be kind,
gentle and loving, even though the people we deal with are not. We are not naïve. We know that others may take advantage of our kindness, mistaking it for weakness. We are encouraged to continue in Christian virtue because, when the world greets kindness with unkindness, we have a Rock and a Fortress, Jesus Christ our Lord. *On Christ, the solid rock, I stand.*

Law and Gospel

Do we then overthrow the law by this faith? ... On the contrary, we uphold the law. (Romans 3:22-31; v. 31).
We hold the banner high and proclaim loudly that the grace of God is available to all sinners—no one is beyond the range of God's grace in Jesus Christ. This does not mean that the law of God has disappeared. The law serves a very good purpose, namely to show us just exactly why we need God's grace. *I thank you, heavenly Father, for the comfort of your grace; in Jesus' Name.*

What Have I Done?

"Those who are well have no need of a physician" (Matthew 9:9-13; v. 12).
Jesus comes for those who really need him. He comes to close the rift that separates us from God and to heal the broken hearts caused by human selfishness, arrogance and thoughtlessness. Those who have never caused God pain, and those who have never brought pain or sadness into someone else's life will have a hard time understanding Jesus. But those who cry, *"What have I done?"* are candidates for the healing balm of the grace of the Lord Jesus. *I have come, Lord Jesus, for an examination.*

Nothing Is Happening

After two days he will revive us; on the third day he will raise us up (Hosea 5:15-6:6; v. 2).
We are happier if we accept life's rhythms as part of God's working among us. Just as plants need time to let the roots grow deeper, so God is working in our lives in hidden ways even when we feel like nothing is happening. Something is always happening! God's Spirit is always at work in our lives, so that "on the third day he will raise us up that we may live before him." *So, Lord, I am just going to wait and see what will happen next.*

COUNTER-INTUITIVE
It depends on faith, in order that the promise may rest on grace (Romans 4:13-25; v. 16).
To live by grace is counter-intuitive. There is always that nagging feeling that comes from somewhere that we need to "do something" to merit God's favor and forgiveness. The reason the gospel is "good news" is just exactly because everything depends on God. For Jesus' sake we are forgiven and have fellowship with God. That is the object and focus of our faith. *Dear God, calm that nagging anxiety about 'doing something,' for Jesus' sake.*

RAGTAG BAND
"Follow me . . . I have come to call not the righteous but sinners" (Matthew 9:9-13; vv. 9, 13).
The company of Jesus' disciples is a ragtag band of people whose broken lives have been mended, restored and completely transformed by the love of God that we encounter in Jesus Christ. We may be tempted to criticize the not-quite-regenerated lives of fellow Christians, but we should remember that, as we follow Jesus, we are all works in progress. *Dear Jesus, I thank you for including me in your ragtag band.*

NO BULL
I will accept no bull from our house (Psalm 50:7-15; v. 9).
This verse is sometimes the object of irreverent merriment. The "bull" the psalmist had in mind was a temple sacrifice offered in lieu of obedience. The "bull" that God does not accept from us is shallow, religious attitudes and actions that we offer instead of genuine commitment to the God who saves us in Jesus Christ. Let there be no "bull" in our religiosity; instead, let there be heartfelt sacrifices of thanksgiving rendered to God for all that God does for us through the grace of our Lord Jesus. *Lord God, I pray that my commitment to you may be genuine in every way; for Jesus' sake.*

A Stone to Stand On
Jesus . . . was handed over to death for our trespasses and was raised for our justification (Romans 4:13-25; v. 25).
This declaration is at once the great stumbling stone and the glory of our faith. Some stub their toes on the inherent and obvious unfairness of the transaction. Why should Jesus suffer for *my sins*? Stand on this stone; don't stumble over it: For Jesus Christ's sake, God has taken away our guilt and made us "just," righteous. This is the glory of God, and the object of our faith. *Help me to believe it, and take it to heart.*

The Urgency
Jesus got up and followed him (Matthew 9:18-26; v. 19).
Matthew the tax collector heard the call of Jesus, got up and followed him. Jesus heard the deep pain of the synagogue leader whose daughter had just died. Jesus got up and followed him! In the midst of every other claim on the time and attention of our Lord Jesus, we should know and believe that Jesus hears our every cry for help, and comes to our aid. Of course, Jesus calls us as well to 'get up and follow.' *Lord Jesus, let me never forget the urgency of your call.*

Names
These are the names of the twelve apostles . . . (Matthew 10:1-4; v. 2).
The Bible is full of names. From Adam and Eve through seemingly endless genealogies to the list of the 12 apostles to the names of early Christians in the New Testament, God's people are not anonymous. We were baptized *by name,* into the Name of our God who is called "Father, Son, and Holy Spirit." *I rejoice that my name is tied to your Name, gracious God.*

God's Kingdom

"... the good news, 'The kingdom of heaven has come near'" (Matthew 10:5-15; v. 7).

We talk about 'the gospel' without always being clear on what we mean. Here is how Jesus understands the term 'good news': God's kingdom is near! God's rule is impinging on the affairs of the world, and impinging on your life and mine. Sin, death and evil are against the wall. Nailed to the wall with no chance for escape! Nailed to the cross of Jesus, we would say. In the end, it is Jesus himself who is the good news, the gospel. *It is good news, indeed, Lord God, when you rule in my life.*

In Trouble

"When they hand you over, do not worry . . ." (Matthew 10:16-23; v. 19).

All of a sudden, we are worried. We thought religion was innocuous, harmless, of the sort 'whatever you believe is private.' Now Jesus warns us 'they will had you over.' Indecisive and uncertain witness will not bother anyone. The clear, certain naming of Jesus, and none other, as Lord, will get us in trouble with the world and even with our own friends. It is at this point that Jesus tells us not to worry. The Spirit will rescue us and give us the response we need. *Dear God, I pray for the courage of a clear witness.*

The Goodness of the Lord

... *the* LORD *is good* (Psalm 100; v. 5).

The psalmist tells us why the joyful noise, the worship, the singing, and the thanksgiving are appropriate: it is because the Lord is good. Conventional wisdom notwithstanding, we don't go to church or Bible study or Sunday school to learn how to be good. We share in the fellowship of God's people because God is good. The joyful noise comes from those who are not good, but who have experienced the goodness of the Lord through the forgiveness of sins. *You only, dear God, are good and the Source of all goodness.*

THE LABORERS ARE FEW
"The harvest is plentiful, but the laborers are few; therefore ask the Lord of the harvest to send out laborers into his harvest" (Matthew 9:35-38; v. 38).
It is estimated that a quarter of the U.S. population under 40 years of age has never set foot in a church for any reason at all. The harvest is plentiful! Jesus commands us to pray that God will raise up laborers. Interestingly, Jesus does not set preconditions. He does not say, for example, 'able, talented, evangelists.' He says nothing about where they will come from. Maybe from our congregation, or maybe from overseas. *Dear God, the harvest is plentiful; please send out laborers; in Jesus' Name.*

FULL HEARTS
God's love has been poured into our hearts through the Holy Spirit (Romans 5:1-8; v. 5).
The jar is full. The only question is where we have stored it. Is it in the back of the cupboard behind the turkey serving dish where it sees daylight once a year? Or is it front and center, where it is opened and used day after day, and even so, never gets used up? Believe this and embrace this for empowerment in every need: Your heart is full of God's love. How did it get there? The Spirit put it there. *What a wonderful surprise, dear God, to find your love already in my heart.*

ENTICED
. . . something like a burning fire . . . (Jeremiah 20:7-13; v. 9).
We did not volunteer to be members of the body of Christ. We were "called, gathered" (*Catechism*); we were "chosen" (*John 15:16*); or, in Jeremiah's words, we were "enticed." Try as we might to escape God's grasp, there is something burning inside that won't give us rest. We will find the peace we need when we finally give in to God and allow God's word free reign in our lives to direct and console us. *I give up. You have found me, again.*

June 24
THE NATIVITY OF SAINT JOHN THE BAPTIST
... the messenger . . . is coming . . . and who can stand when he appears? (Malachi 3:1-4; vv. 1, 2).

When God sends a messenger to prepare the way, we should not be surprised if it causes us discomfort. We long for "the day of the Lord" because the world needs to be made right, and we also need to be renewed and transformed. The messenger will draw our attention to sinfulness wherever it is found, and at the same time point the way to the Redeemer. In Christ, we are finally able to stand. *When your messenger is finished with me, stand me up, O God, in Jesus' Name.*

DAILY DROWNING
. . . our old self was crucified (Romans 6:1-11; v. 6).

Change is not easy, and radical change might even be as violent as a crucifixion. Baptism brings a radical change to our existence. It is nothing less than death and resurrection—death to old self, and newness of life in Christ. Between Sundays we may forget that we have been baptized into the crucified and risen body of Christ. That is why Luther recommends that "the old person in us with all sins and evil desires is to be drowned through daily sorrow for sin and repentance . . ." *How refreshing it is to repent, and then to be forgiven!*

AN OPEN DOOR
No longer enslaved to sin (Romans 6:1-11; v. 6).

Habits are hard to change, as everyone knows. Attitudes walk beside us and we don't even notice. We need to be reminded—daily, according to the *Catechism*—that we are free from the enslaving power of sin. The door is open, the ropes have been cut, the clank and clatter of shackles falling to the ground remind us of our freedom in Christ.

The Lord Jesus dwells in our hearts and is transforming us, teaching us the habits and new attitudes of love for God and neighbor. *Lord Jesus, you have "set me free / from Satan's tyranny / From fear of death and power of sin / From all that plagues my soul within . . ."* (Hans A. Brorson / Oscar R. Overby).

SOMETHING IS STIRRING
. . . dead to sin and alive to God . . . (Romans 6:1-11; v. 11).
Alive to God! Some behaviors in other people provoke a response of irritation and annoyance in us. Certain remarks about politics, or race, or even religion can easily provoke an unhealthy reaction from us. Something else is stirring in our veins, however. It is the presence of God's Spirit poured into our hearts at baptism. Suddenly the Spirit helps us to see that we are dead to the suffocating routine of old attitudes and behaviors, and alive to God in Christ Jesus. *Breathe on me, Breath of God.*

DISAPPEARANCE
. . . consider yourselves dead to sin . . . (Romans 6:1-11; v. 11).
What if anger, greed, jealousy, disrespect, indifference, desire for vengeance and a host of other anti-social behaviors suddenly disappeared from the world? What if these things disappeared from our own lives? This is in fact both the baptismal invitation and the baptismal gift. We have died to sin in the baptismal water, and we are alive to God in Christ Jesus. It is the promise and the gift. *Heavenly Father help me to see my own life from the new perspective.*

AT ODDS WITH THE CULTURE
As for me, my prayer is to you, O LORD (Psalm 69:7-18; v. 13)
Biblical images of God's people being scoffed at, ridiculed, even lowered into a cistern, there "sinking in the mire" (v. 14), perplex us. That is not our experience. However, the things God leads us to

embrace in Christ—justice, righteousness, peace—are at odds with values entrenched in our culture and we are afraid to take up the challenge. It is our own doubts, fears and failure of nerve that mock us! Our prayer to the Lord our God: *Give us the courage to proclaim your new creation!*

LOVING GOD
"Whoever loves son or daughter more than me is not worthy of me" (Matthew 10:24-39; v. 37).

Perhaps there is more grace here than we would have thought. Francesco, age 5, asked his mother, "Who do you love more—me or God?" His mother said, "I love you more, of course." Francesco replied, "I think that is your big mistake." Children who know their parents love God more than anything else will discover their parents' love for them is not in any way diminished. *Gracious God, help me to love you above everything else.*

June 29
SAINT PETER AND SAINT PAUL, APOSTLES
Let no one boast about human leaders . . . whether Paul or Apollos or Cephas [Peter] . . . you belong to Christ (1 Corinthians 3:16-23; vv. 22-23).

If a day is named in honor of luminaries like Peter or Paul it is simply to give God thanks for their lives and witness. Even if these two pillars of the church did not always see eye to eye, we have come to know the grace of God in Christ Jesus through their witness and through the work of innumerable people, living and dead. We pray that God will use our own lives as instruments of blessing for others as well. *To you alone the glory, heavenly Father, for the lives and witness of Peter and Paul.*

THE MESSAGE AND THE MESSENGER
". . . whoever welcomes me . . . welcomes the one who sent me" (Mathew 10:40-42; v. 40).

Those who bear the message about Jesus Christ will be encouraged to know that, while some reject and scorn the Message, *there will be* those who are open and receptive and who will honor the messenger for the sake of the Message. Those who are receptive to the Message about Jesus Christ experience the fellowship of the Holy Trinity, Father, Son and Holy Spirit. *Give power, courage and blessing to my pastor, dear Lord.*

NOTHING TO YAWN AT

. . . from death to life . . . (Romans 6:12-14; v. 13).

God grant that we never find ourselves yawning at the baptismal gift. It is nothing short of miraculous, incredible, and amazing in every respect. By baptism into Christ God has brought us from death to life. Born anew! A second chance at life! Not by our efforts or cleverness but by God's grace. Freed from sin's power to condemn, corrupt and control us, we are alive in ways that only faith in Christ will reveal to us. We are alive in God's new world where things are right, and so there is also peace, and joy. *God, may your baptismal gift keep us wide awake.*

HALLELUJAH!

Happy are the people who know the festal shout (Psalm 89:1-18; v. 15).

After World War II a representative of the Lutheran World Federation, an American pastor, was visiting churches isolated by the war. He went to visit a Hungarian pastor. The American and the Hungarian found they had no common language. They sat in the Hungarian pastor's kitchen, taking sip after sip of a strong fruit beverage, shouting "Hallelujah!" They found their common language. Happy are they who know how to say, Praise the Lord! *and who walk, O LORD, in the light of your countenance.*

OBEDIENCE

. . . obedience from the heart . . . (Romans 6:15-19; v. 17).

Being forced to do something hardens the heart. Doing the same thing because we want to makes the heart glad. God has found a way to gladden our hearts! The grace of the Lord Jesus has freed us from our slavery to sin. The Spirit transforms our stubborn and rebellious hearts into places where there is a desire for God Himself, a desire to please God, and a desire to be a source of blessing through love and service to our neighbor. The Spirit of Christ has given us a new heart. *Grant me joy and peace in willing obedience.*

SANCTIFIED
The advantage you get is sanctification (Romans 6:20-23; v. 22).
If there is resistance to being "sanctified" it is a sign that Old Adam/Eve is still in control. There is no advantage in that. Living for one's self only results in the unending pursuit of something that we cannot define and the feeling of being taken for a fool by the enemy of our soul. To be sanctified is simply to be made into the image of Christ by the Spirit's power. The advantage is we sense God's approval and we experience the joy of Jesus. *Help me to embrace with joy the gift of sanctification.*

FALSE PROPHETS
As for the prophet who prophesies peace . . . (Jeremiah 28:5-9; v.9).
"Dueling Prophets"—it could be the name of a television program, and sometimes it is. One speaks of war, famine and pestilence; the other boldly promises peace. Which one would you point your remote to? A soothing, rather than challenging, message is the one we would probably prefer, but we know from God's truth revealed in Jesus Christ that the cross precedes resurrection, and self-denial comes before glory. *Lord God, by your Spirit help me to discern who is truly speaking your word.*

July 3
SAINT THOMAS, APOSTLE
Thomas answered him, "My Lord and my God!" (John 20:19-31; v. 28).
Doubt and faith are really closer together than we often think. People who claim to be doubters are often believers just waiting for an excuse to commit themselves. The amazing thing about Thomas is that he is

held up as a 'doubter,' and yet his confession of faith is a ringing affirmation of who Jesus is. He is our Lord and God, and it often takes a doubter to point this out to us. *My Lord and my God, support me in my doubts and in my faith.*

SELF-UNDERSTANDING

I do not understand my own actions (Romans 7:15-25; v. 15).

We do not know ourselves as well as we think we do. One of the mysteries of human life is why we do the things we do, especially when the things we do leave us sorrowful or ashamed. Thanks and praise to God who alone understands us and has saved us from ourselves. We are "in Christ" and as such we are a new creation. Self-understanding now focuses on understanding Christ. *Teach me, heavenly Father, the new way of Christ.*

THE LAW

I see . . . another law at war with the law of my mind (Romans 7:15-25; v.23).

The law chiseled in stone on the courthouse lawn is the one we love with our minds but the law that we follow turns out to be the law of sin and death. The law (The Commandments), rightly understood, neither saves us nor makes us better persons. The law shows us our sin and drives us to Christ. Who will deliver me from the law? It is Jesus Christ, the fulfillment of the law, *to whom alone be all glory and honor in the church and among his people, now and forever.*

THE ALLNESS OF 'ALL'

The LORD is good to all (Psalm 145; v. 9).

Even though we consider ourselves theologically enlightened, still there is the idea that, if there is justice at all, rewards and punishments are handed out by God according to one's merits or misdeeds. The amazing thing, however, is that the Lord is good to all. Notice how the word "all" shows up time and again in this psalm. God makes the rain fall on the just and unjust alike, observed Jesus (Matthew 5:45). Praise

God, the Merciful Father and Source of all goodness, for giving us all things by grace, from daily bread to eternal salvation. *You are good to all of us, gracious God. Hallelujah!*

IT IS HE WHO COMES TO US
"Come to me, all you that are weary and are carrying heavy burdens, and I will give you rest" (Matthew 11:28-30; v. 28).
There aren't many who are excluded from this most gracious invitation. Who among us is *not* tired out or does *not* carry a heavy load of anxiety? We should not get absorbed in the mechanics of how this "rest" actually comes into our lives. If we knew, we could do it ourselves. It is Christ's gift to us, and requires simply an open and believing heart. We come to Jesus, but in so doing, we find it is he who comes to us. *Lord Jesus, I believe you will give me rest.*

WEIGHING THE BURDENS
". . . all you that are weary and are carrying heavy burdens . . ." (Matthew 11:25-30; v. 28).
There is no "qualifying" to determine how heavy a burden must be or how weary a person needs to be before seeking the respite Jesus promises. Let every sigh be a prayer; let every deep breath in the face of a new task be a surrender to the need for the power and life of Jesus Christ to see us through. Let every pain, every anxiety, every bit of bad news be an occasion for turning to the Lord Jesus Christ for rest from the myriad forms of this world's weariness. *[sigh . . . deep breath . . .] Lord, have mercy.*

THE YOKE'S ON YOU
"Take my yoke upon you . . ." (Matthew 11:25-30; v. 29).
Yoked to Jesus! It is not a question of being yoked or not. It is a question of which yoke we will accept. What power or force or ideology has us in harness and "teaches" us our values? What is the "way of life" or "life-style" that has us in its thrall? To take the yoke of

Jesus is not only to find rest, but to enter into a commitment to walk with Jesus and learn from him. Pulling the plow, side by side, Jesus will teach us what God's kingdom is all about. *Lord if you pull I will follow.*

AN ALIEN WISDOM

"*. . . learn from me . . .*" (Matthew 11:28-30; v. 29).

What we learn from Jesus is not a series of facts that would be useful to know, not even a special kind of wisdom, although Jesus is eminently quotable. What we learn is a way of life, a way of life given over, heart and soul, to worshiping, honoring, and obeying God. It is a wisdom alien to the world's wisdom because it inevitably will lead to finding one's life by losing it in service to God and neighbor. *Grant that I may be an eager learner.*

PURPOSE, AS A VERB

My word . . . shall not return to me empty, but it shall accomplish that which I purpose, and succeed in the thing for which I sent it (Isaiah 55:10-13; v. 11).

Perhaps one of the reasons "bearing witness" seems to be so hard is that we mistakenly assume that whether people believe or not depends on the force of our eloquence. It is not our word, but God's Word that we speak. What we utter in faithfulness to our Lord Jesus Christ will not be without fruit. God's Word will "succeed in the thing for which I sent it." *May your Word find success in my life.*

UNDERSTANDING THE WORD

"*When anyone hears the word of the kingdom and does not understand it . . .*" (Matthew 13:18-23; v. 18).

We do not understand everything in the Bible. Perhaps we do not always ask the right questions. Try asking the Holy Spirit, What does this say about the Kingdom of God? The "pearl of great price" is the word of how, through Jesus Christ, God rules the world and our own lives, and defeats evil and death. Hang on to this word—don't let go—and God will daily increase and deepen your understanding. *Spirit of God, help me to understand the mystery of your rule.*

SINKING ROOTS
"... *such a person has no root*" (Matthew 13:18-23;v. 21).
Roots are not sunk in one day, but every day is important for the development of a plant's root system. So, too, in one's life in Christ, the enthusiasm of one day will not produce roots deep enough for the long term. Through daily attention to scripture, prayer, and the companionship of other believers, the roots sink deeper and deeper. Then when above ground there is drought, wind or storm, faith does not dry up. *Lord God, make my faith as tenacious as a root.*

CHOSEN!
Happy are those whom you choose (Psalm 65; v. 4).
The happiness of the Christian does not depend on everything turning out conveniently for us. Happiness derives from the fact that we are chosen! Have you heard the word of the gospel of Jesus Christ? You are chosen! Were you grafted into the crucified and risen body of Christ through baptism? You are chosen! Did you just happen to pick up this book after it had been discarded by someone else? You are chosen to experience the grace of God in Jesus Christ! *Gracious God, I feel chosen, and I am happy.*

TOO BUSY
"... *the cares of this world and the lure of wealth choke the word*" (Matthew 13:18-23; v. 22).
Some people boast about how busy they are. Even if it sounds like complaining, it may be bragging disguised as a complaint. There is "call waiting" to carry on two conversations at once. There is the phenomenon of "multi-tasking." We are the over-scheduled

generation. All this busyness, to say nothing of the lure of wealth, leaves no space for the word of God's kingdom. Clear a space for God in your life and see what happens! *Dear God, I guess I'm not really that busy. I am happy to sit here quietly with you.*

FRUITFUL PRODUCTION
". . . the one who hears the word and understands it . . . bears fruit . . ." (Matthew 13:18-23; v. 23).
The kind of understanding Jesus is talking about is not the kind that took theologians a few hundred years to articulate to everyone's satisfaction. The word of God's kingdom is the simple proclamation that, in Jesus Christ God has acted to deliver you and the whole world from sin, death and devil. God rules through the grace of the Lord Jesus. Let this word take root in your soul, learn what it means for you, and you will be surprised at what fruit God produces through you. *Heavenly Father, grant that I may be good soil in your kingdom.*

A PLACE FOR THE MIND
. . . those who live according to the Spirit set their minds on the things of the Spirit (Romans 8:1-8; v. 5).
Thinking about how to get even or using our energy to "get ahead" belong to "the flesh." *We* are in the Spirit, and things of the flesh no longer interest us. The Spirit of God leads us to think of reconciliation and peace making, of loving and befriending the unlovable and the unfriendly. The result of setting our mind on the Spirit is life and peace. *O God, turn the thoughts of my mind Spiritward.*

Waiting for the Lord's Day

V. Still Pentecost

Jesus, still lead on,
Till our rest be won;
And, although the way be cheerless,
We will follow, calm and fearless;
Guide us by thy hand
To our fatherland.

When we seek relief
From a long-felt grief,
When temptations come alluring
Make us patient and enduring;
Show us that bright shore
Where we weep no more.

--Nicolaus Ludwig von Zinzendorf, 1700-1760
tr. Jane Borthwick, 1813-1897

July 22
SAINT MARY MAGDALENE

Mary Magdalene went and announced to the disciples, "I have seen the Lord" (John 20:1-18; v. 18).

Mary Magdalene is one of the heroic, unsung people of the Bible. Standing close to his cross on Good Friday, now coming to the tomb early, what did she expect to do or see? Even when it seemed the mission and purpose of Jesus had been crushed, she was there. Then, in a remarkable twist, as she was immersed in her sorrow and perplexity, Jesus comes to her and calls her by name. Mary Magdalene, apostle to the apostles, is the first to announce the good news of the resurrection. *Lord Jesus, in my perplexity I hear you calling my name.*

The Patient Gardener
"Where did these weeds come from?" (Matthew 13:24-30; v. 27).
Compulsive gardeners can often be found meticulously pulling up weeds that have no place among roses or tomatoes. We wish life in general, or in our family, or even in a Christian congregation could be as perfect as a flower garden. Unfortunately, weeds sprout and grow all over the place, even in our own lives. We can be glad that the Lord is patient with us. If the Lord is slow to judge us, we can be slow to judge others. *Gracious God, I pray for the gift of weed-tolerance.*

July 25
Saint James the Elder, Apostle
"You do not know what you are asking" (Mark 10:35-45; v. 38).
The outdoor sign at a church said, "Come, join the fun." Jesus said, "Take up your cross." James and John thought they deserved places of honor in the kingdom. Followers of Jesus always need to be rescued from misguided notions of discipleship. In the end, being one of the first Christian martyrs was the honor bestowed upon Saint James the Elder. In the meantime, while we await our moment of crisis when our witness is demanded of us, we will pay renewed attention to the servant features of discipleship. *Lord Jesus Christ, I am glad my record of discipleship is not on view. Empower my serving, and grant patience in suffering.*

Dare We Say It?
Abba! (Romans 8:12-17; v. 15)
This strange sounding Aramaic word "Abba" means "Father," or even "Daddy." Such intimacy with God almost seems inappropriate. Nevertheless, the Holy Spirit puts this word on our lips and we are children of God, heirs with Christ of the blessings and richness of our Father's kingdom. We do not judge God the Father on the basis of earthly fathers. Rather, we judge earthly parents on the basis of God, who is "merciful and gracious, slow to anger and abounding in steadfast love and faithfulness." *Abba! Father!*

Waiting for the Lord's Day

UN-DIVISION
Give me an undivided heart (Psalm 86:11-17; v. 11).
There are tugs and pulls for our loyalty and devotion from every direction. Work, family, and other consuming interests, country: these loyalties are mixed together, and where is Jesus Christ in all this? The point is that "mix" is the wrong way of thinking about it. Ultimately there is only one loyalty, to Jesus Christ alone. No one can serve two masters. "Seek first the kingdom of God," Jesus said, and all other needs will take care of themselves. Love for God makes no room for competitors in the undivided heart. *Father in heaven, help me to love you with my whole heart.*

THE COMMUNION OF SINNERS
"... *in gathering the weeds you would uproot the wheat along with them*" (Matthew 13:24-30; v. 29).
We might think that a little weed-pulling will make us a healthier church. Jesus is saying that pulling out the weeds will make us weaker. The church is often a messy place, filled as it is with sinner/saints. We should be grateful that judgment does not occur along the way, else we might find ourselves in the compost bin along with other organic refuse. The Communion of Saints is also the Communion of Sinners, gathered shoulder to shoulder, embracing, uplifting one another, giving thanks for God's tolerance for weeds in the garden. *O God, help me to love my fellow sinners as you love me.*

MOTHER EARTH WAITS
... *the creation itself will be set free from its bondage to decay* (Roans 8:18-25; v. 21).
Natural disasters bring out the inner theologian in everyone, even television news readers. How to explain tsunamis or tornadoes? Sometimes the scientific explanation is best. Shifting tectonic plates or the collision of cold and warm air are more to the point than talk about what God could or could not avert. Even Mother Earth waits,

like the rest of us who deal with evil and tragedy in the human sphere, for the Day of the Lord Jesus Christ and the new creation. *With the creak and groan of this old earth, I, too, pray, Come, Lord Jesus.*

THE BRIGHTNESS
Then the righteous will shine like the sun in the kingdom of their Father (Matthew 13:36-43; v. 43).
What keeps this world from being a dreary place is the brightness of God's righteous people. Our righteousness is the righteousness of Jesus Christ which transforms us so that we are "little Christs" to our neighbor. At baptism we say, "Let your light shine before others that they may see your good works and give glory to your Father in heaven" (Matthew 5:10). *Dear God, grant that I may be a little candle, here, in this place.*

THE PRAYER-CHECKER
We do not know how to pray as we ought (Romans 8:26-39; v. 26).
We say we are unschooled in prayer, as though that were an excuse not to pray. "We do not know how to pray" is a biblical truth, albeit a partial truth. The rest of the truth is this: "The Spirit helps us"! So there is no excuse. Pray without ceasing. The Spirit is the prayer-checker, breathing into our prayers the right words and thoughts so that everything conforms to the will of God. Let there be frequent prayer among us. Since God's Spirit prays with us, we can't go wrong! *Dear God, when I pray sometimes all I can manage is an empty sigh. Your Spirit understands perfectly.*

CONFORMED
. . . predestined to be conformed to the image of his Son (Romans 8:26-39; v. 29).
Some resist the idea of being predestined because they don't trust God to make the right choice. Others might not be keen on it because they are uneasy about being "conformed." It is only our fallenness

Waiting for the Lord's Day

that resists the newness. In our heart of hearts we really do want to be "Christ-like." The bending, shaping, conforming process is only painful to Old Adam/Eve. The new creature that emerges can only give thanks and glory to God for the transformation! *In my heart of hearts, dear God, I really do want transformation.*

PLEASING GOD

With open mouth I pant, longing for your commandments (Psalm 119:129-136; v. 131).

We glorify our personal freedoms to the point of idolatry, but in the end, wandering this way and that in our perfect freedom tires us out and leaves us empty. We can draw up the rules for our own way of life that please us, or we can turn to the God who created us and redeemed us from our mindless wandering to learn what is pleasing to God. We will find that what pleases God also pleases us. *I pray that I may find pleasure in obedience.*

DIVERSIFY!

"The kingdom of heaven is like treasure hidden in a field" (Matthew 13:44-52; v. 44).

The investor acts contrary to the advice from his financial advisor. "Diversify"! the expert said. But this discovery was too great to pass up. He liquidates all his assets—car, house, boat, stocks, golf clubs, everything of value—and trades it in for the rule of God in his life and world. God's rule is revealed in Jesus Christ, where sin and death are conquered and where men and women are transformed into the righteousness of God. *Jesu, priceless Treasure, Source of purest pleasure, Truest friend to me . . . Thine I am, O spotless Lamb, I will . . . ask for nought beside thee.* (Johann Franck, 1618-1677; tr. Catherine Winkworth, 1829-1878)

A STRANGE TURN

"The kingdom of heaven is like a net" (Matthew 13:44-52; v. 47).

Suddenly, Jesus' description of the kingdom takes a strange turn. That the net collects all kinds of fish pleases us. That a selection is made and some are thrown out is scandalous. If it is God's kingdom then we will have to allow God to choose. If we understand that we live by grace, there is no reason for panic or challenge to God's authority. It is precisely the fish who will recognize their unworthiness to be part of the day's catch who belong in the kingdom. *I am grateful for your net that captured me, Lord God.*

Ho, Ho, Ho!

Ho, everyone who thirsts, come to the waters (Isaiah 55:1-5; v. 1).

"Ho" is a Hebrew word that is left untranslated in this reading. It is not so much a word that has a definition as it is an inarticulate sound which represents sorrow or anguish. The prophet yearns to give those who are thirsty the water of life, and for free! but the thirsty do not turn in to take advantage of the offer. Evangelists who offer life in Jesus' name feel the same way about people who are indifferent to God's grace. *Lord God, renew my amazement at your grace.*

Bread

Why do you spend your money for that which is not bread . . ." (Isaiah 55:1-5; v. 2).

How to tell the difference between what is "bread" and what is merely superfluous is the major economic challenge for Christians in the so-called developed world. Garage sales remind us that this is not as easy as we think. "Listen carefully to me," God says through the voice of the prophet. "Your sins are forgiven, you are loved, there is the hope of glory, you have food and shelter. So why do you invest in nothingness?" In body and soul, we are blessed in every way. It is not merely a question of learning to live simply; it is also a question of recognizing the prodigious nature of God's grace. *Thank you, Lord, for the Bread of Life.*

All Ears

Incline your ear . . . (Isaiah 55:1-5; v. 3).

With the television we can turn up the volume because we have the remote in hand. God, however, cannot be manipulated by pushing buttons, so we need to pay attention. For those who are listening, God is speaking, but of course there are other sounds as well. We need to bend the ear and tune in to God' Word. It may be a warning, it may be a reminder, it may be a word that touches a raw nerve. Ultimately, however, God's Word to us is love, joy and peace through Jesus Christ. "Listen so that you may live." *So many voices, Lord, so many choices.*

LOOKING FOR SOMETHING

The eyes of all look to you . . . (Psalm 145:14-21; v. 15).
Sooner or later everyone looks for help. Self-sufficiency has its limits. When funds are scarce, when health is an issue, when conscience pinches, our eyes turn to the Lord of heaven and earth for mercy and relief. In scarcity we become thankful, when we feel a weakness we rely on God our Strength, and when we feel we are needing . . . something . . . but don't quite know what, the grace of the Lord Jesus brings forgiveness of sins and fellowship with God. *Thanks to you, O God, for all your goodness to us, through Christ our Lord.*

APART, BUT NOT ALONE

Jesus . . . withdrew from there . . . to a deserted place by himself (Matthew 14:13-21; v. 13).
Sometimes a person just needs to be alone. Overwhelmed by events or circumstances, sometimes it is a good idea to "withdraw," if even for a few minutes. When we are apart we will discover that we are not alone. The deserted place is filled not only with the thoughts that drove us there but also, and especially, with the presence of Jesus Christ, who promises "My grace is sufficient for you, for power is made perfect in weakness" (2 Corinthians 12:9).

NO MEAGER GIFTS

"Bring them here" (Mathew 14:13-21; v. 18).
A large crowd and virtually no food. Five *bollitos* and two tilapias wouldn't even be enough for Jesus and the Twelve. The needs of our city, not to mention the world, are so great and we have nothing here but a few pitiful resources. Five loaves and two fish seem like nothing but it turns out to be plenty. Our faith (though slight), our gifts of

time, talent and treasure (however modest), our love for God and neighbor (however fickle)—are all more than enough when we obey the command, "Bring them to me." Placing them in the hands of our Lord Jesus, there remains only amazement at what God will do. *Lord, increase our faith!*

ABUNDANCE

. . . twelve baskets full (Matthew 14:13-21; v. 20).

It is fear of not having enough that drives many of our decisions and influences our attitudes. Jesus is not at all worried about scarcity. In the hands of Jesus even a very little turns out to be more than enough. The gospel of Jesus Christ is about abundance, not scarcity. There is more than enough grace to go around for sinners of all kinds. There are more than enough chairs and food for all the odds and ends of humanity that God desires to invite to the Messianic banquet in honor of our Lord Jesus Christ. *God of abundance, deliver me from the fear of not enough.*

You should observe silence, in that manner the word can be uttered and heard within. For surely, if you choose to speak, God must fall silent. There is no better way of serving the Word than by silence, and by listening.
–Johannes Tauler, ca. 1300-1361

SILENCE

. . . a sound of sheer silence (1 Kings 19:9-18; v. 12).

It is an oxymoron. How can silence make a sound? Yet Elijah heard it and stepped out to investigate. Some look for God to work through great winds, earthquakes, or fire, but often God brings about his will and purpose in quieter, less spectacular ways. Here is an invitation to pull back from the rush and energy of life and let God be God. We can never be sure of what we will find in the stillness. It may be simply a time of waiting until things get sorted out. Some people call it discernment. Then, the command: "Go, return on your way." Work and witness continue, empowered by the silence. *Lord, my life is so busy, do I have time for stillness?*

Waiting for the Lord's Day

NO REASON TO FEAR
What are you doing here, Elijah? (1 Kings 19:9-18; v. 13).
The question seems to be a kind of rebuke, but we can understand Elijah's point of view. "They have killed your prophets with the sword," he said, and the possibility that he might be next was the reason for his flight to the mountain of God. Strangely, the answer Elijah gets to his complaint is not one of cloying sympathy. Instead, God sends him on a mission. If we are engaged in what we perceive God is calling us to do, there is no reason not to do it. *Dear God, have you given me a mission or purpose?*

THE MISSION FIELD
The same Lord . . . is generous to all who call on him (Romans 10:5-15; v. 12).
One sainted missionary described evangelism as one beggar telling another beggar where to find bread. It is not the generosity of God's grace in Jesus Christ that is in question. The question is how to make God's generosity known so that people may call on his name to receive what he has promised. The great missionary task, whether the 'field' is across the sea or across the street, is to make Christ known to people who have lost their way. *Lord Jesus, make yourself known to me.*

HOPEFUL WAITING
Restore us again, O God of our salvation (Psalm 85; v. 4).
In the life of faith it is distressing to find that there are times of bleakness when the exuberance seems to have dried up. Some days we do not feel close to God. From time to time we lose sight of the newness of life promised in baptism. Then, "Let me hear what the Lord God will speak, for he will speak peace to his people" (v. 8). Sometimes faith is expressed in exuberant exaltation. Very often faith is revealed in hopeful waiting. *Let me hear what you will speak.*

TOSSED ABOUT
. . . battered by the waves . . . (Matthew 14:22-33; v. 24).
"Against the wind and battered by the waves" is a metaphor that fits too easily into just about everyone's life. It is as true for Christians, individually and collectively, as it is for anyone else. The promise we

cling to as we are tossed about by life's adventure is that "nothing in all creation will be able to separate us from the love of God in Christ Jesus our Lord" (Romans 8:39).

NEW CHALLENGES
They cried out in fear (Matthew 14:22-33; v. 26).
Christian maturity requires adaptability and agility in the face of changing conditions. Whether gradual or sudden, our first instinct is to cry out in fear. What we don't even suspect is that the "ghost" we apprehend as a threat may actually be the Lord Jesus Christ presenting us with new challenges and new calls to faithfulness. In the face of perceived threats, Christian maturity learns to ask, Where is Jesus in this situation? *Where are you, Lord; and where should I be?*

"LORD, SAVE ME"
"Lord, save me!" (Matthew 14:22-33; v. 30).
We will not fault Peter for sinking into the water after only a few steps. Most of us have never taken any steps at all across the water, but all of us have experienced fear and consternation when we notice the strong wind. We will not think less of Peter for crying out, "Lord, save me!" Jesus came for this purpose, to save us from sin, death and the power of evil. In every fear, distress, or pang of conscience we will join Peter in saying, *"Lord, save!"*

GOOD CHRISTIAN PEOPLE
"... *the Pharisees took offense when they heard what you said*" (Matthew 15:10-20; v. 12).
Those we consider 'good Christian people' sometimes react strongly to the word of God that challenges their life style. 'Good Christian people', however, recognize that 'goodness' is always God's goodness, conveyed through the grace of the Lord Jesus. 'Good Christian people' are always open to the stern judgment of the law, because the law shows us our sin and drives us to Christ, where we encounter forgiveness and perfect peace with God. *With all my heart, I*

take refuge in God Most High, the merciful Father, source of all goodness.
(prayer from *The Three Refuges*, Dr. Karl Ludvig Reichelt)

A CLEAN HEART
"What comes out of the mouth proceeds from the heart" (Matthew 15:10-20; v.18).
Words spoken in jest do not always convey that sense. They may reveal a harshness within us that we were not aware of. Our speech and our actions always betray what is in our heart. If we are puzzled about why we do or say the things we do, the answer lies in the heart. Therefore, with David, we pray, *"Create in me a clean heart, O God, and put a new and right spirit within me."*

EVERYTHING BY GRACE
. . . that your way may be known upon earth (Psalm 67; v. 2).
We desire the blessing and grace of God, and we long to see God's face beaming approvingly on us. But all this is not for our sake alone, but for the sake of the world. God blesses us in Jesus Christ, and through this blessing and through our witness God intends for the whole earth to perceive that God gives us all things—life, well-being, and fellowship with God—by grace. *Bless me, gracious God, to be a blessing.*

WHO IS CHOSEN?
A Canaanite woman . . . started shouting . . . (Matthew 15:21-28; v. 22).
The mystery of 'chosenness' is revealed in the agonized cry of this woman. Just as "Abraham believed in the LORD, and the LORD reckoned it to him as righteousness" (Genesis 15:6), so the woman's absolute trust in Jesus revealed her, too, as one of the chosen, in spite of being a "Canaanite." "Woman, great is your faith! Let it be done for you as you wish!" *Dear God, we are all outsiders. Thank you for hearing our cry.*

Knowing One's Place
"... *even the dogs eat the crumbs that fall from their master's table*" (Matthew 15:21-28; v. 27).
"Woman, great is your faith!" Seldom does anyone else receive such great praise from Jesus. In one sense, the woman 'knew her place.' As a foreigner, she had no standing to make a claim on Jesus. On the other hand, if her place was on the periphery, or under the table, even there one can expect something from God. Those who 'know their place' are the ones who find themselves in a new place, at the table, with a fancy place card with their name on it. *We are all grateful for the crumbs that fall from your table, Lord God.*

House of Prayer
My house shall be called a house of prayer for all peoples (Isaiah 56:6-8; v. 7).
Of all the people on earth, Abraham was chosen to be blessed by God, and to be a blessing. "In you all the families on earth shall be blessed" (Genesis 12:3). Through Jesus, Abraham's offspring, God fulfilled the promise. The Lord's house, where we worship the God revealed in Jesus Christ, is for all people, all nations. In the Lord's house human distinctions of nationality, politics, race and culture disappear. All are one in the Lord Jesus. God's ultimate purpose for humanity is not enmity and division but reconciliation and oneness through Jesus Christ. *Widen our vision, dear God, to see all who truly belong in your House of Prayer.*

August 15
Mary, Mother of Our Lord
"... *all generations will call me blessed* (Luke 1:46-55; v. 48).
In the person and body of Mary God is fulfilling the deepest longings of the ages. Those who thought God was distant and uninterested discover that God is close by, so near, Incarnate, in our flesh, through Mary. Mary is "blessed" because through her God became a human being and delivered us from sin and death. It is the desire of Jesus to be incarnated in us, too. "Abide in me and I in you." To this end we may follow the example of blessed Mary. When told that she would

be the mother of the Savior, she said, "Here am I, the servant of the Lord."

Absolute Allegiance

"Who do you say that I am?" (Matthew 16:13-20; v. 15).
Take your time before you answer. What you say may determine the shape of the rest of your life. Peter recognized Jesus as the Christ, the Messiah, the fulfillment of God's promises, and more: God's Son! After the cross and resurrection his disciples will call him Lord: the One to Whom heaven and earth bow down; the One Whom they follow with joyful conviction even to martyrdom. If we name Jesus as Lord he will demand full and absolute allegiance as he leads us from death into life and righteousness. *Dear Jesus, your Spirit has called me by the gospel, and I call you 'Lord.'*

Transformation: Part I
Change

Be transformed (Romans 12:1-8; v. 2).
Let us stipulate that not all change is good. The gospel of Jesus Christ, however, is all about change. We are called to repentance, which is a change of mind. We are called to believe in the gospel, which transforms, or changes, our relationship with God, with each other, and with the world. And the gospel changes us. To acknowledge Jesus as "the Messiah, the Son of the living God," is to invite Jesus to change us. *I pray for the gift to know what is changeable, and what is unchangeable.*

Transformation: Part II
The Objects

Be transformed (Romans 12:1-8; v.2).
We are the objects, not the subjects, of the transformation. It is God the Holy Spirit who will do the transforming because what most needs to be transformed is our unwillingness to undergo the process. Here we see again the radical nature of the gospel of Jesus Christ: a new mind, a new mode of being, attitudes and behaviors springing

from the mind of Christ as though transplanted into the central core of our being. *By your Spirit, open me to the gift of transformation.*

PERFECTLY PROPORTIONED
. . . the measure of faith that God has assigned (Romans 12:1-8; v. 3).

Those who think of themselves as 'strong in faith' are sometimes impatient with others whom they may regard as weak in faith. Everyone has as much faith as they need, according to God's purposes. Just as the body is perfectly balanced and proportioned with individual parts and functions too numerous to mention, so the body of Christ, the community of Christian people, has gifts perfectly proportioned to empower our proclamation, in word and deed, of Jesus, "the Messiah, the Son of the living God." *Nevertheless, Lord, increase my faith.*

A CAUSE FOR REJOICING
We have gifts that differ (Romans 12:1-8; v. 6).

An expert on church dynamics wrote, "Every time you discover that you *don't* have a certain gift it is a cause for rejoicing." No one can do everything. If you don't have the gift of teaching, don't feel bad about declining to lead a Bible study. If you do not have the gift of generosity, don't sit there feeling guilty during the stewardship talk. Instead, ask God to show you the gifts you *do* have, for the body of Christ and glory of God. Every Christian, without exception, has gifts that are meant to be used for building up the body of Christ. *May I not be shy in the use of my gifts.*

HUMILITY
. . . the haughty he perceives from far away (Psalm 138; v. 6).

It seems like such an unimportant thing. Compared to murder or theft or adultery, why would God have an interest in reigning in those who think they are better than everyone else? Twice in one chapter of Romans Paul identifies one of the marks of people who have faith in Christ: they are not haughty. For Jesus, the first step was humiliation, "taking the form of a servant" (Philippians 2). For his disciples as well, the first step is to deny themselves and take up the cross. *How may I serve you, Lord Jesus?*

Rock Music
"*The gates of hell will not prevail*" (Matthew 16:13-20; v. 18).
We "believe" in the holy Christian apostolic church because we do not always see it. The change in generational values, the forces of cultural secularism, the proliferation of do-it-yourself spirituality and build-it-yourself churches all represent challenges to 'church' as we know it. Rock music and slick split screen special effects dazzle some and puzzle others, but however God is shaping and leading his people, we need not fear nor be anxious. If hell itself will not mount a serious challenge to Christ's church, we have nothing to fear from tastes that are not quite ours. *Heavenly Father, sometimes the changes in church confuse and annoy me. Increase my love for fellow believers.*

August 24
Saint Bartholomew, Apostle
When they had entered the city, they went to the room upstairs where they were staying, Peter . . . Bartholomew . . . (Acts 1:13); "*Here is truly an Israelite in whom there is no deceit*" (John 1:47).
Here is a disciple whose identity is somewhat uncertain. He is called 'Bartholomew' in Acts and 'Nathanael' in John. "Can anything good come out of Nazareth?"(John 1:46), he asks. Was he sarcastic, or simply naïve? If we are by nature sarcastic, cynical, or simply naïve, if Christ is in our hearts there will be no deceit. *Lord Jesus, if the scriptural scribes did not get the names right, I am glad you have called me by name.*

Part I
Let Them Deny Themselves . . .
And Take up the Cross
Love one another with mutual affection (Romans 12:9-13; v. 10).
There is not much self-denial in loving someone who is genuinely lovable or who will love you back. Even Gentiles know how to do

that. The cross looms into view when we come face to face with that prickly personality, or the one who makes incessant and needless demands on our time, or the one who really is an enemy. God wins the love of the world through the cross. We participate in God's love when we love those who know not how to love us back. *God, you know who we're talking about. Strength, Lord.*

Part II
LET THEM DENY THEMSELVES ...
AND TAKE UP THE CROSS

Be patient in suffering (Romans 12:9-13; v. 12).

To the sufferer we say, "This is not your cross! Your suffering is Christ's cross." He takes what is ours and makes it his. What he gives us is his Spirit, bringing assurance that we do not suffer alone and that the victory to be revealed will restore all things to perfect wholeness. What we deny ourselves of, in the power of the Spirit, is anger, self-pity, and any right to special treatment. *Free me, Lord God, from impatience.*

Part III
LET THEM DENY THEMSELVES ...
AND TAKE UP THE CROSS

I have trusted in the LORD without wavering (Psalm 26; v. 1).

Perhaps we could make this boast. Or maybe not. It is more likely that we regret the times when faith wavered. To deny oneself and take up the cross is to relinquish all claims that might give us an advantage with God. The vulnerability of the cross reveals itself in our willingness to believe what God promises, righteousness through faith in Christ. To take up the cross is to acknowledge the precarious nature of our faithfulness so that we can rely on the faithfulness of God to forgive, renew and restore. *Steady my wavering faith, Lord.*

Waiting for the Lord's Day

Part IV
LET THEM DENY THEMSELVES...
AND TAKE UP THE CROSS

Bless those who persecute you (Romans 12:14-21; v. 14).
When criticized, a well-known twentieth century philosopher would say, "Thank you for contributing to my self-understanding." When someone gives us a hard time, most of us become at the very least, defensive, or more likely, combative. "Christ died for the ungodly" (Romans 5:6) as unlikely as that seems. By the cross of Christ God desires to bring blessing to a world hostile to God. The cross we take up is the cross that yields to God our desire to get even, to fight back, and what we gain by this is a desire for God's gifts for those who trouble us. *Protect me, O God, from that person who wishes me harm, that I may be empowered to bless and not curse.*

Part V
LET THEM DENY THEMSELVES...
AND TAKE UP THE CROSS

So far as it depends on you, live peaceably with all (Romans 12:14-21; v. 18).
Self-denial often means giving up a 'right' to which we are entitled, giving up an advantage even to our hurt, so as to avoid contention. There are people whose ignorance and misguided views inspire our most reactive wrathful response. The self-denial practicing Christian will walk away from the prospect of a good fight. In any event, the cross of Christ has won all. *Lord, make me an instrument of your peace; in Jesus' Name.*

I AM THERE

"*... where two or three ...*" (Matthew 18:15-20; v. 20).
We know where to find Jesus when we need him. We look to the Lord's Supper where we feel his Touch in, with and under the bread and wine. In the preaching of the gospel Jesus is there. When we feel the water run down our face in the morning we remember that we are baptized into the crucified and risen body of Christ. And, to our surprise, when we sit with a friend or two to talk about our faith,

Jesus is there as well. *God, I am looking for someone to talk about 'faith' with.*

God's Pleasure
I have no pleasure in the death of the wicked (Ezekiel 33:7-11; v. 11).
No dancing in the streets of God's kingdom when tyrants are overthrown, mass murderers hunted down and killed, or heinous criminals executed. On the other hand, there is pleasure in the Triune Divine Life when "the wicked turn from their ways". The prophets, speaking by the Spirit of God, knew this, and Jesus embodies it. God is serious about sin, and pleads with sinners to turn their lives around. God values a spirit of repentance in his people, and delights in forgiveness, for Jesus Christ's sake. *Protect me from vengeful thoughts, dear God.*

Consumed from Within
I have no pleasure in the death of the wicked (Ezekiel 33:7-11; v. 11).
What is repentance, if not rejection of self-destructive attitudes and behaviors that will eat us alive if we don't turn back. We condemn ourselves to be consumed from within when we allow dark thoughts to influence our view of other people. We bring ruin on ourselves if our actions are not wholesome and life-enhancing. It is God's pleasure to forgive our iniquity and redeem our lives from the pit (Psalm 103), for Jesus Christ's sake. *Bless the Lord, O my soul, and all that is within me.*

The Deceptions
See, I have longed for your precepts (Psalm 119:33-40; v. 40).
Since we are willful people, our individual, selfish wills collide, seriously damaging our relationship with each other and with God. God's Spirit helps us to see through the deceptions of Old Adam/Eve, and gives us a desire to know and to do what pleases God. Jesus, God's love in the flesh, is the fulfillment of God's precepts. Our true

desire is to find our identity in Christ, and to be Christ-like. *Dear Jesus, help me to recognize Old Adam/Eve when they show up.*

NEARER NOW
Salvation is nearer now than when we became believers (Romans 13:8-14; v. 11).
We have been waiting for the Lord's Day. In the distance we see it and hear it, and a thrill goes up and down our spine. The Day of the Lord is coming! Sin and evil will disappear. Natural disasters will be a distant, vague memory. The disruptions in our relationships will be healed. We will not be afraid to look anyone in the eye. The salvation that God won in the death and resurrection of Jesus Christ will be unveiled for all to see. That Day is nearer than it has ever been before. *Amen! Come, Lord Jesus!*

NEW CLOTHES
Put on the Lord Jesus Christ and make no provision for the flesh (Romans 13:8-14; v. 14).
In baptism we get a new set of clothes. Our new garment is Christ Himself. We are clothed with the righteousness of Christ. Something has been pulled over our head. Momentarily our view is obstructed. Then the head pokes through and there is light again. But the perspective has changed. The mark of the cross on our brow allows us to see everything from the heights of Calvary. Our sin, our death and our enemy the devil have been conquered. We see our best friends and worst enemies loved equally by God who gave his Son, and the garments of Old Adam/Eve are left behind there on the ground beside the baptismal pool. *Glory to you, our God, glory to you.*

BLUE IN THE FACE
"Seizing him by the throat, he said, 'Pay what you owe'" (Mathew 18:21-35; v. 28).
The behavior of the wicked slave shows us the effect of God's law on our lives. It grabs, it seizes, it chokes, and it won't let go. As rebellious children of God, our debt is too great to even think about repayment. Right when we are turning blue in the face we feel the power of Jesus

Christ, his cross and resurrection, to cast off the deathly grip of (the just) accusation of the law. The intervention of God's grace though Jesus Christ means we can breathe again. *Lord Jesus, I owe you my life.*

A GRUDGE
What if Joseph still bears a grudge? (Genesis 50:15-21; v. 15).
Human relationships are so tricky. Sometimes it is simply a misunderstanding, sometimes it is a serious offense. In either case, the best solution is to fix it. Mutual confession and forgiveness is what 'practical Christianity' is all about. The anxiety about a possible grudge is matched by the relief and exhilaration of a patched up friendship. *Lord, I want to be a practical Christian.*

GOD MEANT IT FOR GOOD
What if Joseph still bears a grudge? (Genesis 50:15-21; v. 15).
This heartwarming and most satisfying story could have turned out differently, "but God meant it for good." A family history worthy of any tabloid newspaper is resolved finally in hugs and tears. Since "we are the Lord's" (Romans 14:8) we are also in this picture. Enabled by God's forgiveness through Jesus Christ, grudges, jealousy, secrets, crimes and misdemeanors, and the fear of our adversaries are washed away in the joy of forgiveness and reconciliation. *Truly, Lord, there is nothing like the joy of reconciliation.*

AS FAR AS THE EAST IS FROM THE WEST
He will not always accuse (Psalm 103; v. 9).
We should not understand "always" to mean that God never accuses. The righteous demands of God's law accuse us of our failure to love God with our whole heart and our neighbors as ourselves. If God "always" accused we would be left in eternal despair. Thanks and praise be to God for grace that removes our transgressions "as far as the east is from the west." For Jesus Christ's sake, we don't get what we deserve, and we get what we don't deserve (v. 10). *Bless the Lord, O my soul!*

September 14
THE HOLY CROSS
For God so loved the world . . . (John 3:13-17; v. 16).
The Holy Cross of Christ stands against a world of vengeance, where every wrong committed needs to be answered in equal measure. Sometimes we worry that God might operate in the same way. The psalmist assures us that God "does not deal with us according to our sins" (Psalm 103:10). Instead, God points us to the cross, the death of the only begotten Son, as the place where all sin, vengeance, and retaliation are themselves put to death. In their place, forgiveness. *In the cross of Christ I glory . . .*

EATING MEAT
Welcome those who are weak in faith (Romans 14:1-6; v. 1).
Eating meat sacrificed in pagan temples does not trouble us. There are, however, more than enough other moral and theological issues to spark debate and stir up emotions. It is important to bear witness to the truth of the gospel, as the Spirit leads us in our understanding. It is also important not "to pass judgment on servants of another" (v. 4). What matters ultimately is that faith in the Lord may come into clearer focus as faith deepens and matures. *Lord, increase my faith.*

LIVING AND DYING
If we live, we live to the Lord (Romans 14:7-12; v. 8).
It is comforting to know that "if we die, we die to the Lord." It is also good to remember that, living, we also "live to the Lord." All our work, activities, and encounters become sacred when we acknowledge the Lord's Presence in everything. We meet Jesus in other people, and they in us. Our work, tasks, errands, are never meaningless, but done to the Lord, they are holy tasks, and will bring blessing. Even a time of sitting quietly alone can be offered up to God, because Jesus promised to be with us always *In Jesus' Name I begin my next task.*

WHAT IS FAIR?
"Are you envious because I am generous?" (Matthew 20:1-16; v. 15).
The maddening thing about God is his Generosity. No labor union would agree to the system of payment outlined by Jesus in this parable, and certainly no landowner would dream of such a thing. Jesus gives a New Meaning to the concept of fairness. In the economy of the kingdom of heaven the measure of all things is the Generosity of God. Just as we were about to register a protest we remembered that we, too, are beneficiaries of God's Generosity. *My love for you is always meager compared to your generosity, O Lord.*

LIVING AND DYING
Living is Christ and dying is gain (Philippians 1:21-26; v. 21).
Sometimes we understand this verse in a backwards way, as though living were gain and in dying we meet Christ. We will never be able to embrace the "dying is gain" until we first grasp that living is Christ. Having a 'good day' does not depend upon meeting a cheerful clerk in the store. It is the grace and presence of the Lord Jesus Christ that fills every corner of our lives, making even hard times come alive with the Awareness that passes all understanding. *Let there be life!*

September 21
SAINT MATTHEW, APOSTLE AND EVANGELIST
"Follow me" (Matthew 9:9-13; v. 9).
We admire Matthew and the other disciples for their eagerness to follow Jesus. But if our only reaction is admiration, we miss the point. Jesus also calls us to follow him, to take his words seriously, to take up the cross through self-denial so that the life of Christ Jesus germinates and grows in us as well. Unless we are those who have "no need of a physician," Jesus came to draw us also into the power of his life and his righteousness. *In the footsteps of Matthew and the rest, I do wish to follow you, Lord Jesus Christ.*

Waiting for the Lord's Day

THANK YOU

Every day I will bless you and praise your name forever and ever (Psalm 145; v. 2).

One spiritual giant has suggested that the most fundamental prayer is "Thank you." That is the essence of blessing and praising God. We awake and find we still have life and breath and we bless and praise God for it. Drinking a cup of coffee, the blessings and praises ascent on high. We go about our daily routine, we do our work, we meet people, in all the sights and sounds we say, *"Thank you, Lord!"* It goes on forever and ever. *Again and again we say, Thank you!*

A WORTHY MANNER

Only, live your life in a manner worthy of the gospel of Christ (Philippians 1:21-30; v. 27).

A "manner worthy of the gospel" surely applies to questions of morals and ethics. But in the context of the parable of the landowner who hired laborers at various times during the day, the "manner worthy of the gospel" also means to enter into God's joy when another person is touched by grace. If it is God's pleasure to welcome and forgive even latecomers, then as people who have been hired early in the morning it is our pleasure as well. *I am grateful for employment under your rule, gracious God.*

A CONSTANT TURNING

Only, live your life in a manner worthy of the gospel of Christ (Philippians 1:21-30; v. 27).

If only we could remember, all the time! every day! –that Christ has put to death Old Adam/Eve and raised us up as a New Creation. Then we might have something to brag about. Old Adam/Eve always wants to point to some great 'worthiness' in us. Even if we are declared 'saints' by God's grace, we are still 'sinners' and the thing most worthy of the gospel is a constant turning for repentance and renewal. The life "worthy of the gospel" always points back to Christ. *I praise you, Lord Christ, for making me worthy.*

Waiting for the Lord's Day

REALLY ANGRY
Is it right for you to be angry? (Jonah 3:10-4:11).

"Yes," answered petulant Jonah, "angry enough to die." Like Jonah we would often rather judge and condemn than forgive and welcome. However, our attitude has no influence on how God will deal with other people. God will be gracious, whether that makes us happy or not. We might as well be happy and participate in God's pleasure.
Our Father in heaven . . . forgive us . . . as we have been forgiven.

VI. Even So, Come, Lord Jesus

My Lord and my God,
Take everything from me
Which prevents me from coming to you.

My Lord and my God,
Give everything to me
Which helps me draw near to you.

My Lord and my God,
Take me away from myself
And give me entirely to you, yourself.

--a German prayer

JESUS IS LORD

Jesus Christ is Lord (Philippians 2:1-13; v. 11).
If Jesus is Lord, then we are not lords and ladies of our own lives. It is a bold affirmation to say, with the Spirit's help, Jesus is Lord. Bolder than we imagine, because we thus state our ultimate and singular allegiance. Moreover, that grand, glorious, almighty and supremely mysterious Figure in the Old Testament named LORD has now been revealed in the flesh. Jesus Christ is the LORD. Jesus Christ is nothing less than the Almighty God made visible. *My Lord and my God!*

September 29
SAINT MICHAEL AND ALL ANGELS
And war broke out in heaven; Michael and his angels fought against the dragon . . . that ancient serpent . . . the deceiver of the whole world . . . was thrown down . . . (Revelation 12:7-12; vv. 7, 9).

God's mighty messengers the angels are on our side! Even though there is anguish in our lives (as Daniel says [12:3]), there is **no despair!** The one who accuses us of sin, of disobedience and unfaithfulness to God has been thrown down and conquered by the Lord Jesus Christ. Rejoice then, heaven and earth, and all heavenly and earthly creatures! For the sake of Jesus Christ you are considered righteous. In the power of Jesus Christ, you are able to live a righteous life. *With angels and archangels we praise your Name, O Lord God!*

THE NAME
. . . at the name of Jesus every knee should bend (Philippians 2:1-13; v. 10).

"How sweet the name of Jesus sounds!" intones the hymn. When we hear The Name we feel a frisson of wonder and delight throughout our bodies. In Jesus God touches us; in Jesus God becomes real; and in Jesus we experience God as love. The very name "Jesus!" brings all this to mind. The name of Jesus overwhelms us and our own power leaves us. Wobbly knees bend, and in that weakness we discover a strength, a power not our own, surging though us and raising us up again. That power is the Name of Jesus. *With utmost reverence I say, Lord Jesus Christ.*

GOD'S NATURE
Be mindful of your mercy, O Lord (Psalm 25:1-9; v. 6).

Our nature is to remember our sins and forget that God is merciful. In this psalm we pray that God will be true to his nature, remembering to be merciful and forgetting our sins. Past mercies lead us to count on God for today. Our memory extends backwards even to the sins of our youth. God's mercy takes care of the past and draws us forward into Christ. In Jesus Christ we are ever mindful of God's mercy. *Help me to believe in the forgiveness of sins.*

GOD'S PLEASURE
Turn, then, and live (Ezekiel 18:25-32; v. 32).
Prophets seem to be happy only when they are scowling. The prophet, however, reflects God's will and purpose. God's pleasure is not to condemn, but to save us from sin and death. The scowl on the prophet's face is not for judgment, but reflects consternation and perplexity, as though to ask, "Why do you reject God's call to receive mercy?" "Turn and live" is fulfilled in the words of Jesus, "Repent and believe in the gospel." *In your face, Lord Jesus, I see God's mercy.*

A RIDDLE
"Neither will I tell you . . ." (Matthew 21:23-27; v. 27).
We'll have to figure this one out on our own. The dilemma for the chief priests and elders is our dilemma as well. Does Jesus Christ embody the power, love and presence of God in our world, or not? The answer we give will either please God, or it will please 'the crowd.' We can seldom please both. If we take a stand for Jesus, we risk alienating friends and neighbors, even people we love dearly. Maturity means taking a stand. No one can do it for us. *Heavenly Father, I believe your love and power are made real in Christ.*

FRUITLESS
"He sent his slaves to collect his produce [fruits] (Matthew 21:33-46; v. 34).
Justification by grace though faith in Christ (apart from 'works') is not an excuse for branches bare of fruit. The same Spirit that brings us to faith in Christ is the Spirit that desires to produce the fruits of love, joy, peace, patience, etc. (Galatians 5:22). Scripture is harsh on 'the tree that does not bear good fruit.' If we feel fruitless, it is only a matter of opening ourselves to the Spirit of Jesus Christ, who, to our great surprise, is able to bring forth the fruits that we have desired. *I need a few deep breaths of your Spirit, Lord Christ.*

Waiting for the Lord's Day

KNOWING CHRIST

I want to know Christ (Philippians 3:7-14; v. 10).

Better than self-righteousness, better than self-promotion, better than favorable comparisons with other people, the righteousness of Christ is worth giving up everything else for. "If you know Christ well, it is enough, even if you know nothing else; if you do not know Christ, it is nothing, even if you know all else" (Life motto of Johannes Bugenhagen [1485-1558], Luther's friend and co-worker). *I want to know Christ.*

THE VINE

Why have you broken down its walls? (Psalm 80:7-15; v.12).

Christendom isn't what it used to be. The walls have been breached, and the usual occupants of the city have fled, some to various forms of 'spirituality' or 'spiritual, not religious,' some to ecclesial bodies with a very short history. It may seem that "the boar from the forest is ravaging the vine." The Vine, however, is Jesus Christ. If we have been sleeping while on watch and allowed the walls to be broken into, our rebuilding will be to abide in the Vine, for "apart from me you can do nothing" (John 15:5). *We turn again and again to you, O Christ the Vine.*

HOW LONG?

O LORD God of hosts, how long will you be angry with your people's prayers? (Psalm 80; v. 4).

We pray once or twice. And still nothing has changed, it seems. Our prayer is righteous and wholesome, and still God does not act. In the end we come face to face with the sovereignty of God. We pray our hearts out and then we can only wait, acknowledging that we can do nothing until the brightness of God's face shines on us, and then we shall be saved. *O God, I pour out my heart to you. And then I wait.*

KNOWING CHRIST

I want to know Christ (Philippians 3:7-14; v. 10).

Over time we grow comfortable with our religious and spiritual customs. The danger is that we may confuse our comfortable customs with the real thing. Spiritual customs that one finds congenial "are

Waiting for the Lord's Day

only a shadow of what is to come, but the substance belongs to Christ" (Colossians 2:17). To know Christ is to know both glory and pain, abasement and exaltation. Sorrow for misbehavior as well as scorn for bearing the Name will lead us again to Christ Jesus where rivers of grace forgive and comfort. *Nevertheless, I still want to know Christ.*

THE THINGS GOD LOVES

I press on . . . because Christ Jesus has made me his own (Philippians 3:7-14; v. 12).

Every day is a turning point. Every day is an opportunity to turn in faith to Jesus Christ in order to be clothed in righteousness once again. "And being found in Christ" with a righteousness not our own, we are able to pay attention to God, and to love the things that God loves. Justice, love for God's world and God's people, peace among tribes and nations, are high on the list of things that God loves. *Dear God, I want to love what you love.*

NOT WORTHY

. . . they made light of it . . . (Matthew 22:1-10; v. 5).

When invitations to a royal wedding are highly coveted, it is inconceivable that any who received one would laugh it off. In addition to the prestige, think of the free food. Only an exalted ego and bloated sense of self-importance would lead a person to make light of such an opportunity. Those who think they are too good for the wedding feast of God's Son are declared unworthy. Let them go about their business as though nothing else mattered. God's will, however, is to fil the banquet hall, one way or another, with the "good" and the "bad". *I am holding on tightly to my invitation, grateful to be included.*

ALL TOGETHER

My brothers and sisters, whom I love and long for . . . (Philippians 4:1-9; v. 1).

You can pray, sing, and read Scripture in the solitude of your prayer closet, but out of the solitude comes a deep yearning for the company of fellow believers in Christ. Whether they are the "good" or the "bad," there is joy in seeing everyone else gathered for worship. Hearers of the Word and fellow guests at the wedding banquet of our Lord Jesus Christ, it is our joy to be with our Lord, all together. *Gracious God, how very wonderful it is when your people gather on the Lord's Day.*

REJOICING SPONTANEOUSLY

Rejoice always! (Philippians 4:1-9; v. 4).
The beautiful banner hanging in the chancel commanding worshipers to "Rejoice!" is not always met with a cheerful heart. Sometimes we just don't feel like it. Sitting in prison, Paul has apostolic authority to command Christians to rejoice always. It is not our current situation—however favorable or unfavorable it seems to be—which gives us joy, but the underlying condition of being 'in Christ'. Since we are invited to the marriage feast of God's Son, rejoicing spontaneously happens anytime and possibly despite the circumstances. For Paul, faith in Jesus Christ meant prison. Whatever self-denial and the cross hold in store for us, being 'in Christ' always occasions rejoicing. *When I feel sorry for myself, remind me again, dear God, that I am 'in Christ.'*

THE TABLE

You prepare a table . . . (Psalm 23; v. 5).
The table is set and the bowls steam with hot food. It is the perfect ending to a day that, with assorted highs and lows, has left us tired, but above all, hungry. In God's presence, and against the background of sin, death, and evil—our ancient and contemporary enemies—a table has been set, a banquet, a cup running over. It is the grace of the Lord Jesus Christ for forgiveness, life and salvation. *Lord Jesus, you are always the Host and I the guest.*

EVEN OUR ENEMIES

. . . in the presence of my enemies (Psalm 23: v. 5).
Pious Christians may say they have no enemies. In the honesty of our hearts, however, we can pretty easily name a few. If we are feasting

and enjoying the never-empty cup, there may be some short term satisfaction in seeing our enemies looking on wistfully or jealously. Perhaps God's purpose is to move our hearts to include even our enemies in the banquet. The never-empty cup convinces us that, if those looking through the window are invited in, there will still be enough for all of us. *Enlarge my heart, O God, to include all whom you love.*

AGAIN AND AGAIN
Again I will say, Rejoice (Philippians 4:1-9; v. 4).
There are times in life when once is not enough. When a reconciliation has taken place, one "Thank you, Jesus!" is never enough. When we hear, again and again, that God's love for us is persistent in spite of our behavior or situation, no amount of genetic reticence can suppress the joy. When we are aware of God's Presence even in the ordinary or difficult things the sun beams on our faces and there is no concealing the inner joy. *Lord, I pray for a cheerful countenance.*

October 18
SAINT LUKE, EVANGELIST
"You are witnesses of these things" (Luke 24:44-53; v. 48).
Thank God for the witness of Saint Luke! Only Luke tells us these things: the songs of Mary, Zechariah and Simeon; the familiar Christmas story; Jesus' announcement in Nazareth that he was "anointed . . . to bring good news to the poor"; the parables of the lost sheep, coin, and (prodigal) son. We praise God for all faithful witnesses, living and dead, who have declared to us the richness of the work of Christ and by the Holy Spirit, convinced us to put our trust in the Lord Jesus Christ. *Heavenly Father, may my life be a witness to your grace, in Jesus' Name.*

TAXES
"Is it lawful to pay taxes to the emperor, nor not?" (Matthew 22:15-22; v. 17).
Poke around the edges of the taxation question and you will hear outbursts of indignation. The complaint is that taxes deprive us of our "hard earned money." Not counting waste or corruption, taxes, in

principle at least, are for the common good. But of course the issue in this text is not really about taxes. The question was a trick to get Jesus involved in political questions. The kingdom of God is bigger than politics, bigger even and more important than any earthly empire. What belongs to God is our undivided love, allegiance and service. Our whole hearted obedience to God points us to the Second Greatest Commandment, to love our neighbor as ourselves. Paying taxes for the common good is one way of loving our neighbor. *Heavenly Father, grant us good government and honest leaders.*

NO OTHER GOD
I am the LORD, and there is no other; besides me there is no god (Isaiah 45:1-7; v. 5).
Jesus put it this way: "No one can serve two masters" (Matthew 6:24). There are a host of attractions and allegiances eager to absorb our time, resources and energy. Some, like "family," or even "country," seem unassailably noble. Others, like the gladiatorial contests in the fall, turn out to be empty calories. There is no order or ranking of allegiances. There can only be one, just God alone. "I am the LORD, and there is no other." We have one Master, the God reveled to us in Jesus Christ. *Increase my love for you, dear God.*

SONGS OLD AND NEW
O sing to the LORD a new song! (Psalm 96; v. 1).
Songs of the faith are dear and precious to us. Perhaps we even know some of them by heart. They hold memories and make past experiences come to life again every time we sing them. Praise God for old songs. Praise God for new songs as well. God is continually at work in us, renewing us, helping us to defeat old Adam/Eve, bringing us into the light of the new creation in Christ. A new song can help us see the new thing that God is up to. *O God, you invented sound. Give me a song to praise you today.*

Music is the heartbeat of God.
--John Ylvisaker

Waiting for the Lord's Day

TREMBLING

Worship the LORD in holy splendor; tremble before him, all the earth (Psalm 96; v. 9).

We must never become so familiar with God that we lose our capacity to tremble in God's Presence. What inspires awe and causes us to "tremble, tremble, tremble" is not that we have managed to come into the presence of the transcendent glory and splendor of God, but that the glorious Word of God becomes human and comes into our presence. *Glory to you, our God, glory to you.*

RESISTANCE AND TRANSFORMATION

God has chosen you . . . not in word only but in power and in the Holy Spirit (1 Thessalonians 1:1-10; vv. 4, 5).

Those were the days! We were ecstatic in those days when we first learned that God has rescued us from sin, death and devil by the death and resurrection of Jesus Christ. It wasn't by convincing words or stunning light shows but it was the power of the Holy Spirit that opened our hearts, melted away resistance, and transformed incompatible personalities into people whose hearts were filled with love for God and for one another. *Dear God, renew my enthusiasm and joy, for Jesus' sake.*

IDOLS

And how you turned from idols (1 Thessalonians 1:1-10; v. 9).

We are surprised to learn that we have "turned from idols," because the idols that tempt us are not necessarily chiseled in wood or stone. Power, whether economic or political; a business or profession; a way of life or lifestyle; wealth or the desire for it—all these can lead to idolatry. In the end these pursuits mock us silently because they provide neither forgiveness of sin, nor life, nor salvation—the very gifts that the God revealed in Jesus Christ gives us by grace through faith. *Unveil my idols, Sovereign Lord.*

Flattery: Part I
OUR APPEAL
. . . we never came with words of flattery . . . (1 Thessalonians 2:1-8; v. 5).

In an age where many people no longer feel the need for church membership, churches have taken to advertising. One congregation invited people saying theirs was a church "where intelligent people gather." Others make appeals based on fulfilling perceived 'needs.' No one, it seems, dares to invite people to "deny yourself, take up the cross and follow Jesus." The Apostle says, "We never came with words of flattery." *Lord God, I have no other 'need' than to be gathered into your grace.*

Flattery: Part II
CHARMING
. . . we never came with words of flattery . . . (1 Thessalonians 2:1-8; v. 5).

The gospel is good news, but not because it flatters us by affirming our way of life, life-style, or because we are so charming. There can only be good news if we allow the Lord Jesus Christ to be our righteousness. Being 'right with God' begins by acknowledging we are not right with God, but Christ makes us right, by grace, through faith. *I believe that your grace changes me.*

Flattery: Part III
OUR APPEAL
. . . we never came with words of flattery . . . (1 Thessalonians 2:1-8; v. 5).

The gospel does not first tell people that they are 'OK' just as they are. The gospel first of all draws a dismal picture of our human reality. People captivated by sin, death and evil need to be rescued. Since we are helpless to do it ourselves, the gospel tells us that God transforms sinners into righteous people through the death and resurrection of Jesus Christ. *God be praised for transformation!*

Waiting for the Lord's Day

THE HARDEST ONE
"You shall love the Lord your God with all your heart . . ." (Matthew 22:34-40; v. 37).
The First and Greatest Commandment is also the hardest. So many forces, attractions, causes and institutions have their arms outstretched, all grasping for a large piece of our heart. God is God and there is no other. God is God all day and all night and all week long. Even when our hearts are in some other place, God is
attentive to our needs for love, forgiveness, help and comfort. It is for this reason that God asks for our whole heart. *I praise you, O God, for your unfailing love.*

A COMPLEX INDIVIDUAL
"You shall love your neighbor as yourself" (Matthew 22:34-40; v. 39). Self-love has been promoted quite successfully. Now it is time to turn our attention to the main thrust of this Second Greatest Commandment, our neighbor. The neighbor is a complex individual, just as we are. He or she was profoundly marked by unique experiences growing up. Our neighbor has hopes and frustrations. Our neighbor is given to fits of anger, surges of jealousy, periods of moodiness. Our neighbor's politics may be very different from our own. What our neighbor desperately needs on this day is our love. *Help me to see my unlovable neighbor in a new way.*

THE CHANGE OF SEASONS
. . . their fruit in its season (Psalm 1; v. 3).
Fruit trees give thanks when their season is over. Production requires enormous, exhausting stores of energy. The change of seasons is for rest and renewal. The chief change of season for us is the Lord's Day! Here God's Word and the Body and Blood of Christ give us respite from the constant demands to be producing Christian charity and an articulate witness all the time! Empowered by the grace of the Lord Jesus, when the time comes to love and serve our neighbor, we will be ready. *Dear Lord, I thank you for the Day of Rest.*

Waiting for the Lord's Day

October 28
SAINT SIMON (NOT SIMON PETER) AND SAINT JUDAS (NOT ISCARIOT—SO THEY CALL HIM JUDE), APOSTLES

"Lord, how is it that you will reveal yourself to us and not to the world?" (John 14:21-27; v. 22).
This is a day for obscure disciples, just like us. Judas (not Iscariot) asks a question. As is Jesus' custom, the answer he gives is not direct, but it *is* an answer. It is just exactly when the disciples of Jesus "keep his word" and the Father and Son through the indwelling Holy Spirit "make their home with them" that Jesus is revealed to the world. *I thank you, Lord God, that like Simon and Jude, you have made yourself known to me, and through me to the world.*

October 31
REFORMATION DAY
NOTHING "TO DO"

What becomes of boasting? (Romans 3:19-28; v. 27).
'Righteousness' is not a word everyone thinks about every day, but it is something we all want, whether we are even aware of the idea or not. Since we are incapable of standing before God with a clear conscience we are relieved to learn that righteousness is never an achievement; it is always given. We believe the promise that on account of Jesus Christ we are right with God. Even that faith, which stands against all human reason and logic, is a gift. There is nothing left "to do"—except to return thanks with love for God and neighbor. *Amazing grace, how sweet the sound / That saved a wretch like me!* (John Newton, 1725-1807)

LET GO AND LET GOD

"Everyone who commits sin is a slave to sin" (John 8:31-36; v. 34).
Our fierce commitment to 'freedom' is offended by these words of Jesus. We do not like to feel helpless. Valiantly we maintain the possibility that 'today we can do better.' Instead, what the gospel proposes is to let Jesus be our Savior. If we 'let go and let God' Jesus will defend us from sin and evil. He will forgive, and the indwelling

Holy Spirit will enable us to live as people bound now to the way of God rather than to sin. *Jesus Christ my Savior, you restore my true nature.*

THERE IS A RIVER

There is a river whose streams make glad the city of God (Psalm 46; v. 4).

From the roaring and foaming waters of the sea suddenly there is a gently flowing river in Jerusalem. There is no river in Jerusalem, of course, so the psalmist invites our imagination. In Ezekiel's vision of the New Jerusalem and the new temple, there is also a river (Ezekiel 47:1). The seer of Patmos also saw it, now flowing from the throne of God (Revelation 22:1). This river is the Presence of God, to calm anxious spirits, and to bring life and healing to the nations. For all souls, troubled, fearful, tossed by life's turbulence, there is a river. God's Presence flows into us by the Spirit of Jesus Christ. *My soul longs for the healing of the nations.*

November 1
ALL SAINTS DAY

What we will be has not yet been revealed (1 John 3:1-3; v. 2).

As much as we love this life, there is that shadow of finitude hovering over all. On the other side there is the promise of resurrection, a promise and idea that baffles human imagination. We do not know what it will look like. We believe in the resurrection of the body, but what kind of body? We need not be jealous of those saintly examples of faithfulness who have gone before us, who have already beheld the glory. The promise will be fulfilled for all of us, in God's own time. *Great and amazing are your deeds, Lord God the Almighty* (Revelation 15:3).

SOMEONE WE KNOW

Who are these? (Revelation 7:9-17; v. 13).

If we look closely we may see someone we know. The one who gave all for love's sake but was never appreciated may find herself in this picture. The child who always went to school hungry now, at last, experiences fullness. The person who struggled with faith and doubts

Waiting for the Lord's Day

and temptations all his life now sees clearly! Those who were abused and bullied will be there, but it may surprise us to find our enemies there as well. The abusers and bullies, whether they know it or not, also long to be free of their demons. Life is full of ordeals, some of them great indeed. *Blessing and glory to God who gives the victory through Jesus Christ.*

REVERENCE
O fear the LORD, you his holy ones (Psalm 34:1-10; v. 9).
It is not that we are 'afraid', but we are reverent. By the blood of the Lamb we have been made holy. Mindful of our inherent unworthiness, we come before the throne by the grace of the Lord Jesus. We are reverent, amazed that a sinful person has been invited into the holy precincts of the righteous God. We bow low, grateful for all that comes by grace for our material and spiritual well-being. *I will bless the Lord at all times* (v. 1).

NO DISTINCTIONS
. . . a great multitude . . . from every nation (Revelation 7:9-17; v. 9).
In God's view there is no "Most Favored Nation" status. The work of Jesus Christ is to reconcile all people to God, and neighbor to neighbor. God's will is that "all nations" will come to know the grace of the Lord Jesus and become his disciples (Matthew 28:20). Making distinctions among nations is a characteristic of our old nature. Recognizing that there is "neither Jew nor Greek" (Galatians 3:28) is a feature of God's new creation. *You are worthy, our Lord and God, to receive glory and honor and power, for you created all things . . .* (4:11).

A BLESSING
"Blessed are those who mourn" (Matthew 5:1-12; v. 4).
Here God's future is revealed ahead of time. In the present we mourn the deaths of people we love. Jesus pronounces a blessing on the bereaved. It is not by any means to ignore or deny the weight of grief. Rather, it is God's last word spoken already. Not grief or sadness, but resurrection and life, are God's final word, pronounced in the resurrection of Jesus Christ. *Amen! Blessing and glory and wisdom and thanksgiving and honor and power and might be to our God forever and ever! Amen.*

Waiting for the Lord's Day

THY KINGDOM COME

Alas for you who desire the day of the Lord! (Amos 5:18-24; v. 18).
We pray "Thy kingdom come." We know that, whatever else it means, on that day Jesus will come to "judge the living and the dead." Passage into the newness that God promises implies judgment of what is unworthy in us and in or world. This is the "Alas!" the prophet refers to. The "Day of the Lord" also promises that all will be made new. Against that Day we claim the grace of the Lord Jesus Christ for transformation. *Thy kingdom come, and may it come to us as well.*

HOPE EXPRESSED

We do not want you to be uninformed . . . (1 Thessalonians 4:13-18; v. 13).
The glorious End of All Things, and the New Creation promised by God, is beyond the capacity of mere words to explain or describe. Hope is best expressed artistically. Our ears thrill to the sound of God's trumpet, for example. Or, a painting as large as the sky will tell us that the clouds will bring Christ to us and us to Christ. This vision shapes our hope. We are clear about what faith teaches. We believe in the resurrection of the body, without trying to describe it. And satisfied with just the words we believe that Jesus will come again and that we will be with the Lord forever. *Amen! Come, Lord Jesus!*

AN END TO GLOATING

Let those who say, "Aha, aha!" turn back because of their shame (Psalm 70; v. 3).
No one likes a gloater. One gains the upper hand and says, "Aha!" And the vanquished look for a way to get even in order to say, "Aha!" right back. When we bear the sharp pain of humiliation, Jesus is humiliated with us. With the psalmist we look to Jesus, "You are my help and my deliverer." In Jesus, there is forgiveness, reconciliation, peace, and an end to gloating. *You, Lord, are my help and my deliverer.*

THE WISE

". . . the wise took flasks of oil with their lamps" (Matthew 25:1-13; v. 3).
We want to be ready for the Lord's coming, of course, but we also want to be ready for whatever discipleship will require of us every

Waiting for the Lord's Day

day. We keep our lamps burning bright by attending to the Means of Grace: Word, Sacrament, and Prayer. We do not fill ourselves; we are filled, by the grace of God. Our hands, hearts and minds are open to God's Spirit to keep the flame of faith burning brightly in our lives. *"Give me oil in my lamp, keep me burning!"*

THE END
". . . you know neither the day nor the hour" (Matthew 25:1-13; v. 13).
Strange to say, it is often those who think they know Scripture best who, contrary to what Scripture teaches, work out elaborate schemes to predict the End of All Things. Let us take Jesus at his word. The Lord will come when God says it is time. Meanwhile, today is a day of grace to be received in joy and lived by faith in Jesus Christ. *This day, too, is glorious. And I am grateful to be a part of it.*

RESURRECTION
The dead in Christ will rise . . . (1 Thessalonians 4:13-18; v. 16).
We can only speculate about what happens when we die. We should not get overly imaginative about such thigs. We have this promise: nothing, not even death, can separate us from the love of God in Christ Jesus (Romans 8). And this one: the dead in Christ will rise. The faith of the Church, expressed in the Creed, puts it this way: "We believe . . . in the resurrection of the body and the life everlasting." *Keep me grounded, Lord God, in the reality of daily discipleship.*

RIDICULE AND REJECTION
"I was afraid . . ." (Matthew 25:14-30; v. 25).
How we envy those who are not afraid! They dare to let their Christianity show. They dare to challenge the underlying assumptions of political and economic systems. They dare to risk the ridicule and rejection of friends and colleagues by their witness. How we envy those who dare to confront evil wherever they find it. Before the Righteous Judge we will tremble and bewail our timidity. Let us dig up the gift that is ours before disaster comes, and put it to use. *Give me grace to let my Christianity show.*

Waiting for the Lord's Day

ENCOURAGEMENT
Encourage one another . . . (1 Thessalonians 5:1-11; v. 11).
A team on the field of play will not win many games if some scurry off to avoid speaking with their teammates. The world's enmity and disunity sometimes work their way into the church as well. Our encouragement is just exactly that disunity and enmity will not last forever. Jesus is coming! The Day of the Lord is at hand! The jealousies, anger, resentments that exist in the world as well as in the church will be forever swallowed up in the consummation of God's redemptive plan in Jesus Christ. Our encouragement is that Christ died for the church as well as for the world. *I pray for my congregation. Help us to build each other up in love.*

I'M (NOT) COUNTING
So teach us to count our days . . . (Psalm 90; v. 12).
365 times (your age) plus a day for each leap year, plus a few months since your last birthday. We do not dare make the calculation. We are here for so short a time and then we are gone. Only God is immortal. Even a splendid tombstone is not immune to extremes of weather, much less to pigeons. The wisdom that we gain from this dismal exercise is to acknowledge the goodness of our Creator, the incalculable value of each day, and the wonder of the promise of resurrection to eternal life though Jesus Christ. *I praise you, eternal God, for the splendor of this day.*

GIFTS
"*. . . to each according to his ability*" (Matthew 25:14-30; v. 15).
God will not give us more gifts—spiritual or natural—than we can handle! We may feel swamped at times. We may feel as though everything depends on us. It is important to recognize the difference between our work and God's work. God's work is to save the world. Everything depends on God! Confident of this, our work is to use talents, skills and spiritual capabilities to love and serve our neighbor. God will never give us more of this work than we can handle. *A burden has been lifted from my shoulders, Lord.*

Waiting for the Lord's Day

DESTINY

God has destined us . . . for salvation (1 Thessalonians 5:1-11; v. 9).
God wants to save us from sin, death and devil. This is God's purpose for us and our destiny in Christ. Here is a truth we can grab onto and believe with all our heart, and live according to our faith: in Christ God has forgiven our sin and freed us from its power over us. In Christ God promises that death is not final, but will be swallowed up in resurrection. And while evil apparently flourishes unchecked in the world, sentence has been pronounced and the verdict is righteousness through Jesus Christ. *I believe that I am saved by your grace, Lord God.*

THIS OLD EARTH

A thousand years in your sight . . . (Psalm 90; v. 4).
The world is old; our life is short, but God is eternal. Our old earth carries the secrets of past eons, while our appearance here is brief. We rest in the One Who Was even before the mountains were pushed up and the One Who Will Be long after 'heaven and earth pass away.' Jesus reveals the God of eternity to be the God who forgives and continually makes us new, even if life is short. *Lord, you are my dwelling place now and forever.*

NO AMBIGUITY

". . . hungry . . . thirsty . . . a stranger . . ." (Matthew 25:31-46; vv. 35 et al.).
We long for the coming of Christ on that glorious Lord's Day! Or at least we say we do, as long as it does not inconvenience us. Many have their nose buried in the obscure parts of Scripture trying to divine the day and hour. While we wait for That Day, Jesus points our noses in a different direction. There we see the hungry, the needy, the imprisoned and the foreigners with whom Jesus has identified himself. "When you did it, or did not do it to the least of these, you did, or did not do it, to me." There is no ambiguity here for people looking for a Mission or Purpose in Life. *Gracious Lord Jesus Christ, open my heart and bend my will to serve you in my neighbor's needs.*

Waiting for the Lord's Day

BEGGARS

"Come, you that are blessed by my Father . . ." (Mathew 25:31-46; v. 34).
What a wonderful surprise! The righteous had no idea of their own righteousness. The parable reminds us that Jesus is all around us, and needy. Jesus needs to be fed, clothed, housed, visited and welcomed. In the face of overwhelming neediness in this world, our response will always be inadequate. In our own need for righteousness (that is, our need for God), we discover that Jesus has become one of us, too, and exchanged our neediness for his righteousness. According to one story, a note found in Martin Luther's coat after his death said, "We are all beggars, this is true." *And in you, Lord Christ, we are all blessed.*

COME, LORD JESUS

". . . when was it we saw you a stranger . . ." (Matthew 25:31-46; vv. 24, 38).
We are glad to see members of our family pull into the driveway, but the hungry, the thirsty, the strange—these are the ones we do not want to see ringing our doorbells on Thanksgiving Day. "Come, Lord Jesus, be our guest," we pray, but Jesus is already among us, incognito, hidden in those unwelcome guests. Since the secret is out, we know where to find Jesus without having to invite or search for him. *Lord, I acknowledge my reluctance to find you in those who are unwelcome. I can only say, enlarge my heart.*

THANKSGIVING DAY

Then one of them, when he saw that he was healed, turned back, praising God with a loud voice (Luke 17:11-19; v. 15).
One of ten had his wits about him sufficiently to recognize the greatness of what happened to him. Let our praise of God always be effusive. Whether we are grateful for great things or small, let our praise of God be full throated and hearty! *Bless the Lord, O my soul . . . and do not forget his benefits.*

CASUAL SUNDAY

Let us worship and bow down (Psalm 95; v. 6).
Some bow down literally, and others bow in their hearts when they come into the House of the Living God. Faith returns to worship for

continual renewal and awakening. The gladness in the Lord's house is generated not only in the embrace of fellow Christians who welcome us, but especially in fellowship with God in the awe and mystery of worship. If we understand ourselves to be, really and truly, in the Presence of the Living God, worship can never be casual. *Holy, holy, holy! Lord God almighty! Heaven and earth are full of your majesty.*

That Power

. . . that you may know . . . the immeasurable greatness of his power (Ephesians 1:15-23; vv. 18,19).

It is easy to underestimate the power of God. Even hearts hardened by a lifetime of disappointments can be melted by God's love. God is able to ignite a love for God even in deadened consciences. Suddenly freed from oppressive attitudes and behaviors, we are surprised by That Power. One day we find ourselves talking about Jesus with a friend. Astonished, we wonder how and when we started 'witnessing'! Never underestimate the power of God. *Empower my witness and service, for Jesus Christ's sake.*

Saint Andrew's Day

"We have found the Messiah" (John 1:35-42; v. 41).

The Sunday closest to Saint Andrew's Day is the First Sunday in Advent. Saint Andrew thus leads the way into the new church year by announcing to his brother Peter, and to us, "We have found the Messiah." This in turn is the theme for everything we Christians do. To the skeptics, the indifferent, the self-sufficient and to the scoffers we say, "We have found the Messiah." Evangelism is not coercion, but proclamation and invitation. To all Jesus himself says, "Come and see." *Praise, glory and honor to you, O God, through Christ our Lord, in the power of the Holy Spirit, one God, now and unto the ages of ages.*

www.ingramcontent.com/pod-product-compliance
Lightning Source LLC
LaVergne TN
LVHW011423080426
835512LV00005B/223